Introducing the IBM PC*jr*™

Unshelling the Peanut

by

Andrew M. Seybold

Howard W. Sams & Co., Inc.
4300 WEST 62ND ST. INDIANAPOLIS, INDIANA 46268 USA

FIRST EDITION
FIRST PRINTING—1983

International Standard Book Number: 0-672-22317-1
Library of Congress Catalog Card Number: 83-51538

Edited by *Stan DeGulis*
Illustrated by *Eddie Greaser*
Typography by *Graphic Typesetting Service,
    Los Angeles*

Printed in the United States of America.

PREFACE

The microcomputer industry was alive with rumors of the IBM computer code-named "Peanut" for over a year before its introduction. Never before had industry analysts, reporters, and potential home computer buyers alike anticipated the introduction of a new machine with such fervor.

Months before its introduction in November, 1983, articles about IBM's Peanut, now known as the PC*jr*™, appeared in trade journals and newspapers across the country. The day that the new computer was introduced in New York, the story was carried by every television network news program. The PC*jr*™ even appeared as the lead story on the *Today* show the following day.

The PC*jr*™ is an exciting product. It opens new vistas for personal computer users. But the PC*jr*™ is not a major leap forward in technology; rather, it's the result of harvesting the best of available technology. It is truly a pint-sized PC, but with added attractions: two cartridge slots for Read Only Memory (ROM) modules that are used to add other programs such as BASIC and LOGO, a detached cordless keyboard, and keys specially designed for rugged operation.

It will appeal to students and to anyone who plans to use it either for household duties or to run a small home business. It will also appeal to the businessperson who uses a PC or XT at the office and wants to continue work at home.

As you read this book, you will learn not only how the PC*jr*™ works and what you can do with it, but also why you probably want it. You will find out IBM's plans for improving communication and information retrieval and why the PC*jr*™ plays an important role in those plans. You will discover the interesting method IBM used to design the PC*jr*™ keys and how infrared transmitters and receivers form a communication link between the keyboard and console.

The purpose of this book is to introduce IBM's new computer to you. It explains in an easy-to-read manner what changes the PC*jr*™ has brought about in the home computer market and what they mean. It tells you whom the PC*jr*™ was designed for and how you can use it. This book gives you the important information you need on today's most important computer—the IBM PC*jr*™.

ANDREW M. SEYBOLD

CONTENTS

ACKNOWLEDGMENTS

This book, like the product it discusses, is not the work of a single person. It is, rather, the result of long hard hours of dedicated research, writing, editing, and production by many very talented people.

Among these people are Carl Warren, the Western Regional Manager for Howard W. Sams, who worked by my side through this entire project, offering sage advice and untiring dedication, and showing all of us we could complete this project on time.

My staff, Mel Samples and Travis Johnson, who sifted through mounds of notes, documents, and often conflicting reports, and who picked up the pieces and carried on when exhaustion crept over us.

Eddie Greaser, the man who took our primitive drawings and cryptic notes and returned a short time later with real drawings.

John Obst, manager of Howard W. Sams' editorial department who flew to Los Angeles to serve as liaison, project coordinator, and general ombudsman.

Katy Williams, secretary extrordinaire, who devoted her time both graciously and productively to this project, and who kept all of us going with her constant words of encouragement.

Stan DeGulis, who served as editor and mentor, and wove the text and artwork together so skillfully, as well as Bennett Derman and his staff at Graphic Typesetting Service in Los Angeles, who produced typesetting and page composition in a matter of days.

My son Drew, who assumed the role of "gofer" and acting head of household during this project, and my father John, who provided insight into the many facets of writing and skillfully blending words into a finished work.

And finally, a group of people I have not met—the production staff at Howard Sams Publishing in Indianapolis, who responded to our deadlines and produced the final product in record time.

These were the key players in this exciting and rewarding effort. We, all of us, worked like a well oiled machine to produce the book you are about to read. There were others too, who contributed to this book in their own way. They know who they are, and know that I am grateful for their contribution, even though their names cannot appear here.

FOREWORD

No other American industry has been marked by such fascinating products, rapid growth, and general excitement as the microcomputer industry.

The birth of this industry is usually associated with a 1975 article in *Popular Electronics* (now known as *Computers & Electronics*) that described a microcomputer system. In reality, it was born many years before. The industry began in 1947 with the creativity and genius of William Shockley, who created the transistor, and Robert Noyce, founder of Intel Corporation, along with Texas Instrument's Jack St. Clair Kilby, who created the integrated circuit techniques that led to the microprocessor—the heart of modern-day microcomputers.

The exciting discoveries of these chip designers led other far-sighted men such as Ed Roberts, the founder of Micro Instrumentation and Telemetry Systems, to harvest the power of the microprocessor and create the first microcomputer system, the Altair 8800. When this machine appeared on the 1975 cover of *Popular Electronics*, no one fully realized that the genie in the bottle had been unleashed.

Quickly, new companies sprang up—Imsai, Processor Technology, Osborne, and Xitan, to name a few. And just as quickly, many companies faded away, with newer ones taking their place. During these growth years, however, one corporate giant stood at the ready. It watched the progress of the industry and planned the product that would change it overnight. The company was, of course, IBM. The product was the IBM PC. The entry by IBM into the market at last gave the microcomputer a sense of legitimacy; it was now "okay" to buy one for the corporate office.

The microcomputer industry has recently entered another "shake-out" period. Computer companies, while not dropping like flies, are having their share of difficulty. Several have already gone out of business and many more are on shaky ground. No one really knows who the survivors will be, and no one is sure which segment of the large computer market will see the next spurt of activity. One thing that is certain, however, is that "Big Blue," as IBM is affectionately known, will be one of the survivors—probably the leader in this field for years to come.

With the PC*jr*™, Big Blue seems to have done it again. IBM has introduced to the industry not only its new creation, but new excitement and new promises. The PC*jr*™ brings the computer home.

Will the PC*jr*™ be to the home market what the PC and XT have become to the business market? The answer, on the surface, seems to be a resounding "yes." But why? Does it take only a product with the name "IBM" on it to insure success? Or will the public demand that the product also be worthy of their attention? IBM has entered a market area in which it has no experience. Will people accept its entry into the home computer/hobbyist field, or will the PC*jr*™ be rejected for some other machine? As more and more information about the PC*jr*™ becomes available, the pieces of this puzzle will begin to fit together. The entire computer industry is watching for the final picture.

Why did IBM enter this market? Many companies before it tried and succeeded, but many others failed in their attempt. Why did this corporate giant choose to tred where others have failed? The answer lies in the basic premise that today's computer hobbyist is tomorrow's corporate computer user.

For many years, colleges have taught computer programming using systems leased from IBM at greatly reduced rates, often times less than the same system installed in the business world. The benefit to IBM was in the number of graduates who, having become familiar and comfortable with Big Blue, specified an IBM computer when they needed one in the business world. Continuing this trend, college students today are able to purchase PCs or XTs at discounts not available in the business world. Now IBM has embarked on a new campaign, no longer content to grow loyalists at the college level.

Why not build IBM loyalty much earlier? The home computer market affords the opportunity to do just that. Apple, for example, has long recognized the younger generation is important to its future. But Apple's product line currently ends at the high end of the microcomputer market with the LISA. Once a need is established for a minicomputer or a mainframe, the Apple loyalist has nowhere to turn. If, however, the next generation grows up with a PC*jr*™, they can move up to a PC or XT, an IBM minicomputer, and finally an IBM mainframe system. And if these systems are designed to communicate with one another, the progression becomes that much easier to make.

PCs and XTs that communicate and share data with mainframe computers are already a reality. The next logical step is to provide inexpensive access to this same network from the home. What better way to capture the home computer market than to offer a product that provides entertainment and education in the home and that also gives access to systems in use in the business world?

So expect to see more surprises from IBM. The PC*jr*™ is a logical extension in the computer marketplace; it is also most probably part of a master plan at IBM. A Local Area Network (LAN) system to tie the PC and XT into the world of the "big" computers could well be the next announcement from IBM. And don't be surprised if the PC*jr*™ is included in that network.

The PC*jr*™ should gain a strong foothold in the microcomputer market. Like the PC and the XT before it, it will cause a major change in the industry. New magazines will be born, entrepreneurs will search for the ideal add-on product, and scores of existing companies will rush to the marketplace with every conceivable enhancement product for the PC*jr*™. Within the next few months, expect hundreds of companies to be clamoring for the aftersale dollars that the PC*jr*™ will generate. From special desks to advanced memory and display cards, each product will tout something that you cannot live without.

Adam Osborne envisioned a computer on every desk, replacing all the typewriters of the world. IBM must envision a PC*jr*™ in every home, linked to an IBM computer in every office.

CHAPTER 1

WHAT IS THE PCjr™?

Another Personal Computer? Just what the world needs! You may wonder why the PCjr™ is any different from the scores of others computers designed for the first-time home user. Should you be impressed just because it has the name "IBM" on it? Or, more importantly, if you have an IBM PC or XT at the office, can you bring work home and continue it on your PCjr™?

Given all of the available choices, there should be more than just the name to get you excited. It's not a bad reason, but there are many other reasons that make PCjr™ a good buy. We will reveal, bit by bit, (pun intended) the features that make PCjr™ more than just a toy on which to play games.

HISTORY IN THE MAKING

When IBM announced the IBM PC in July, 1981, it was the first personal computer to employ the Intel 16-bit microprocessor instead of the then-standard 8-bit microprocessor. The personal computer quickly moved from being something geared primarily to the hobbyist, to an important office machine. With the PCjr™ IBM has now brought down the cost and size but kept the performance high. The fact that the PCjr™ can address much more memory than its 8-bit predecessors is an important point. In the world of computers, this is a case where more really is better.

But what does more memory really mean? Let's look at it in more basic terms.

The 8-bit systems can address up to 64,000 locations in RAM (random access memory), while a 16-bit system can theoretically address up to 64,000 times 64,000 locations, or 4,096,000,000 pieces of information! In practice, 16-bit processors can access up to 896,000 locations in RAM (we will call that 896K for short, and let K represent thousands). That is still a lot of memory—14 times what an 8-bit system can handle. What does this mean for the computer user? For one thing it means more computing power and speed. A major limiting factor in the processing speed of a computer is the number of times the system must search for instructions and/or data on a mass storage device such as a floppy or hard disk. By having more addressable memory available, larger programs and more instructions can be stored in the actual operating space of the computer where access time is faster.

To put this in practical terms, consider a word processing application. In a typical 8-bit system, you might be able to store the program and five pages of text in the 64K internal memory. (If the 8-bit machine has more than 64K available, do not be fooled: the computer can only use 64K at any one time; it cannot truly access all 128K at once.) If you try to make changes or corrections beyond the five pages available in memory, the computer would have to store the existing material onto a disk or tape and then access the storage device again to read in the new material. All of this takes time and reduces the effeciency of the computer. With a 16-bit system, using 128K of RAM, you can probably store the entire program plus 15 pages of text. Obviously, you could then move around anywhere within those 15 pages without the computer having to access the disk for additional pages. Moreover, calculations take less time, spreadsheets can be larger, and the alphabetical sorting of lists can be accomplished much faster.

Maybe business applications don't interest you. Consider games for a moment. If all of the creatures needed for the game are running around inside your memory, (the computer's memory, that is) they can move faster and more smoothly across the screen, and the coordination of sound to their movement is more realistic. Looking at the same thing in another dimension, game programs for 16-bit computers are more nearly like their arcade cousins than the 8-bit versions of the same program. As a general rule, any operation that can be accomplished in memory will be faster than if the operation requires additional disk access for more data or program segments.

Until the advent of the PC*jr*™, 16-bit machines were pretty much limited to business uses. The main reason is cost. Even though the PC and XT cost two- to six-thousand dollars, they offer a great deal for the money. They are easily justified in an office where just a few years ago a word processor cost ten thousand dollars or more. But most home users are not ready to spend this much money in order to play games.

ENTER THE PC*jr*™

With the introduction of the PC*jr*™, IBM has brought the price of 16-bit machines within the reach of the home user while still keeping most of their power. For the first time, most of the power normally found in business

Fig. 1-1.

computers is readily available to the home computer hobbyist, game player, educator, and programmer.

Just as the PC and XT created a whole new business machine industry, the PC*jr*™ is already creating an industry where super-sophisticated games, educational software, and communications are the rule, rather than the exception.

Limitations on home computers that once were acceptable are no longer. The home user, much like the business professional before him, has become more demanding. IBM has given us the PC*jr*™, a high performance, low cost computer that bridges the gap between a fully functional home computer, and a low-end business system. The market niche filled by this system is actually more than one niche.

Mom and Dad can now purchase a computer for their own use as well as the children's. It can balance the checkbook, prepare a tax return, and keep track of golf scores (do computers lie?), plan menus, keep track of appointments, and help find what you are looking for at the push of a button.

The kids, after seeing other kids on TV do everything from changing their school records (not recommended for the novice), to fighting crime with a computer will definitely be on your side. And how can you fight the idea that everyone has a computer in their future? You have just been waiting for the right time and the right system to come along. After all, it is important that your children be exposed to this wonderful new world of computers. Why they can even play most of their favorite games without feeding it an endless stream of quarters!

Because it is offered in two versions (see below), the PCjr™ can play many different roles in the world of home computing. For the beginner, it represents the state of the art in microcomputers. For the tinkerer, it represents a exciting new challenge, and for the family it represents the most complete home system available today. For small business applications, the IBM PCjr™ is certainly more powerful than most systems that compete with it in price. The small business owner can take advantage of computer technology at little more than the cost of a game. The manager of a company can now do at home some of the scheduling, planning, and letter writing that is currently done in the office until the wee hours of the morning.

BUT WHAT DO I GET?

The IBM PCjr™ is available in two different models. The first is called the entry model, Fig. 1-2. It is a basic computer with keyboard, 64K of memory, a separate power transformer, and two cartridge slots. The second is the enhanced system—a grown-up version of the entry model. Its special features include expanded memory (128K), an 80-column display, and a floppy disk drive (Fig. 1-3). Both models are designed around the same microprocessor used in the IBM PC and XT. Either one can be interfaced to a cassette tape for storing programs, and a total of 14 connectors on the back of either unit allows connection to a multitude of optional devices.

Some of the key points that set this system apart from other comparable units on the market today include:

- Intel 8088 microprocessor
- 64K ROM (Read Only Memory) including 32K of cassette BASIC
- 62-key cordless keyboard
- Two program cartridge slots
- Desktop transformer
- 64K dynamic RAM (16K dedicated to video buffer)
- 128K of RAM in the enhanced version
- Serial port
- Audible alarm
- Sound subsystem

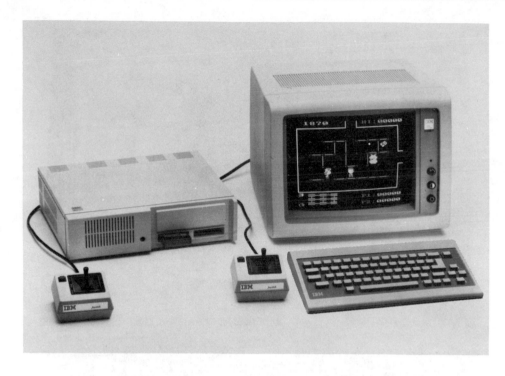

Fig. 1-2. **Entry model PC*jr*™ with joysticks, keyboard and color monitor.**

- Cassette interface
- Joystick interface
- Keyboard cord interface
- Modem interface
- Diskette interface
- Video/Graphics subsystem
- Direct drive and composite video output
- Parallel port for printer adapter
- 9-level interrupt support

IBM has also provided a wide range of add-on options to increase the utility of both models of the PC*jr*™ even more. Let's look at some of the options:

- Joysticks (up to two) —several different types available to suit your trigger finger
- Thermal printer—to permit you to share the results of your labors without a computer at hand

Fig. 1-3. **View of the PC*jr*™ system board with memory expansion, internal modem, and disk drive (enhanced version).**

- Communications modem—to connect to the rest of the computer world, including databases and information services
- Light pen interface—to allow manipulation of text or graphics on the screen by just pointing to it (with some programs)
- Cassette interface cable—to connect to a cassette tape recorder to store data
- Parallel interface adapter—to make the PC*jr*™ compatible with many of the more popular printers
- Serial (RS232C) interface cable—to connect to many popular serial devices, including some printers
- Keyboard cord—to eliminate problems of interference in an area with more than one computer.
- Keyboard overlays—to customize the keyboard for different applications.

Table 1-1 PC*jr*™ Feature Comparison

	PC*jr*™	IBM PC	IBM XT
Floppy Disk Drive	1	2	1*
Hard Disk Storage	no	no	1
Total Memory			
On System Board	128K	128K	256K
Total Expansion	128K	896K	896K
Keyboard Keys	62	83	83
Serial Ports	1	OPT	OPT
Monitors Supported			
Color TV Set	yes	yes	yes
Color Monitor	yes	yes	yes
Monochrome	no	yes	yes
Monitor			
Composite Video	yes	yes	yes
Printers Supported			
Graphics	optional	optional	optional
Compact	optional	optional	optional
Color	no	optional	optional
Typical Prices	$1269	$2798	$5325

* Carrying case—to secure and protect the system during storage or transport
* Modulated video output—to permit the use of a standard TV as a display

The following options for the IBM PC and XT are *not* available for the PC*jr*™:

8087 Co-processor for math functions

Monochrome display adapter

Dual disk drives

Bisynchronous communications adapter

SDLC communications adapter

Hard disk drive (Winchester)

The PC*jr*™ video capabilities support three different types of displays —a modulated output for standard TV, and, for monochrome or color monitors, either composite or direct video. The differences are explained in Chapter 4.

Still with us? Then let's explore the sounds that the PC*jr*™ can make. Unlike most microcomputers on the market today, the PC*jr*™ has no internal speaker (only an alarm is built in). Instead of building it in, IBM treats the sound generation function as a separate subsystem of the overall computer. If you are using a home television for a display, the sound will be generated through the TV speaker, otherwise you will need an amplifier and speaker that functions independently of the monitor.

The sound subsystem is software controlled and is capable of generating three simultaneous voices. This gives the computer the ability to emulate many different types of sounds—from the typical computer beeps to much more sophisicated sound effects used in games. Your first experience with the PC*jr*™'s sound effects will probably be with a commercial program that takes advantage of them. But at some point you may want to try your hand a creating your own sounds. Chapter 5 explores the world of BASIC, a language used to communicate with the PC*jr*™, and the special macro language that controls the sound system.

A CLOSE-UP LOOK

The Cordless Keyboard that uses infrared transmission is the most novel item in the PC*jr*™'s repertoire, Fig. 1-4. With only one function key, it provides with its 62 keys, all of the flexibility of the PC's 83-key keyboard. It accomplishes this feat by using a "smart" keyboard that assigns keys to perform multiple functions. It is a low-profile unit that uses carbon contact rubber dome keys with full travel on a standard typewriter layout. The result is an extremely comfortable "touch." The keyboard is adjustable to two tilt positions, 5° in the standard position and 12° with the legs extended.

In the infrared mode, the keyboard is powered four AA-size batteries. The operator (that's you) may move the keyboard up to 20 feet away from the system unit, as long as you don't wander too far from directly in front of the system. An optional cord is available that permits direct connection

Fig. 1-4.   The PC*jr*™ keyboard.

of the keyboard to the system unit, but it limits your mobility with the keyboard to an area immediately adjacent to the computer. The cord should only be necessary to prevent interference when more than one system is in use in the same area.

The System Unit of both models is identical, (Fig. 1-5). It is approximately 14 inches wide, 11 inches deep, 4 inches high, and weighs in at 6 pounds without the disk drive, or 9 pounds with it. As previously mentioned, the PC*jr*™ comes with two cartridge slots (ports) to take advantage of software (firmware) provided on cartridges. An I/O expansion bus allows for connection to up to 18 additional peripherals. The system unit can be purchased as the entry level version and can be upgraded later by the user, or it can be purchased off the shelf as the enhanced version. There are two additions to the entry-level version that perform the upgrade. The first is the a floppy disk drive, and the second is a combination display and memory expansion module.

The Power Supply/Transformer is a step down transformer, as IBM describes it, providing 33 watts of 60 volt-amps of power.

The power transformer is connected to the main system unit with a 10-foot long power cord and weighs just under 3 pounds. Considering the size, weight, and cord length, this "desktop transformer" might better be called an under-the-desk power supply and weighs just under 3 pounds. This "desktop" transformer has a 10-foot power cord. The size, weight, and cord length would seem to indicate that this is really an under-the-desk power supply.

Fig. 1-5.　**Front view of the system unit.**

The Memory and Display Expansion is the option that expands the basic PC*jr*™ memory (64K) to the maximum permissible in the machine (128K), making it the same as the the enhanced version (Fig. 1-6). In addition, it provides support for 80-column text and high density video display. This memory expansion, by using the 44-pin memory expansion slot on the system board, is the only one supported by the system. The memory expansion does not require reconfiguring the system to recognize the increased memory.

The Compact Printer is a lightweight thermal printer (Fig. 1-7) with all-points-addressable graphics that was designed to interface with the PC*jr*™ (a special adapter cable allows you to use the printer with the IBM PC or XT). The serial interface (a modified RS232C) is accomplished through PC*jr*™'s asynchronous communications port at 1200 bits per second using an 8-bit ASCII protocol (2 stop bits, no parity). The printer has a 256-character buffer and is rated a 50 cps (characters per second) for text, although the printer's real output is typically only 25 cps. It accepts cut-sheet, fan-fold, or roll paper up to 8.5 inches wide and has 4 different text print modes:

Fig. 1-6.   **Memory and display expansion module.**

Fig. 1-7. **IBM thermal printer.**

- Standard mode at 80 characters per line (10 cpi)
- Double-width mode at 40 characters per line (5 cpi)
- Compressed mode at 136 characters per line (17.5 cpi)
- Compressed double-width mode at 68 characters per line (8.75 cpi)

The line spacing is programmable to either 6 or 9 lines per inch. The character density is a 5 × 7 dot matrix (560 dots per line × 8 dots high for graphics). The printer ROM character set consists of 191 characters, including the standard 128 ASCII characters.

The Disk Drive that is standard with the enhanced version and is an option with the entry system, is a 5¼-inch, half-height, double-sided, double-density, 360K unit (Fig. 1-8). It utilizes the same disk format (48 tracks per inch, 40 tracks per side) as both the PC and the XT. The PC*jr*™'s system unit has room for only one drive to be mounted internally, which is all the system supports at the present time. However, the drive is in addition to the cassette interface and the cartridge ports. A new disk operating system (DOS 2.1) is part of the PC*jr*™ release. Special timing requirements of the disk drive used in PC*jr*™ make this new release necessary. DOS 2.1 is compatible

Fig. 1-8. **System unit with disk drive.**

with the PC and XT that use the earlier DOS 1.1 or DOS 2.0 versions, but the PC*jr*™ will only operate using DOS 2.1.

The Internal Modem plugs directly into the motherboard (Fig. 1-9) and does not compete with other peripherals for the system RS232C serial port. The modem is capable of both 110- and 300-baud asynchronous communications in full- or half-duplex mode, and contains a loop-back feature to facilitate diagnostic testing. The serial communiciation characteristics, including 7- or 8-bit character length, even, odd, or no parity, stop bit, and baud rate are fully programmable. Additional features include:

- Dial, ring-back, and busy tone detection
- Line break detection
- Prioritized interrupt system controls
- Overdial
- Call progress reporting
- DTMF (TouchTone™) or dial pulse dialing
- Auto or manual answer and originate

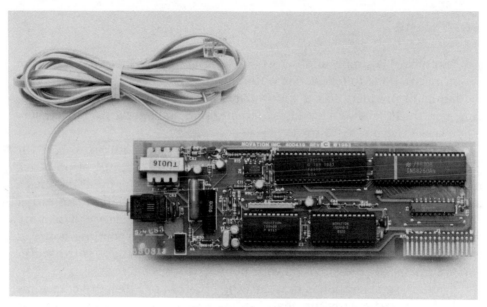

Fig. 1-9.   **Internal modem card.**

The internal modem is approved under part 68 of the FCC (Federal Communications Commission) rules for direct connection to telephone lines and comes with a modular phone jack. Most telephone companies require that you notify them before you connect the modem to their lines. Their tariffs give them the right to know whenever you connect anything except one of their telephones to their lines.

The modem permits the PC*jr*™ to "talk" over telephone lines to other computers. Calling any of the timeshare computers such as the Source[sm] or CompuServe will give you access to everything from computer dating services to airline schedules and reservation, from Dow Jones stock market information to computer shopping services. Additionally, if you have an IBM PC or other type of computer at work that is equipped with a modem, you can call directly to that system and make use of the files it contains. Just think, you can surprise the boss by walking in on Monday morning and already knowing the sales statistics for last week and having the shipping schedule for this week!

The Carrying Case is for those who need to transport their computer from place to place and want to feel secure that they have done everything they can to protect it. The case accepts the system unit, the parallel printer attachment, up to four program cartridges, the TV connector, keyboard, power transformer and cord, and up to five diskettes. This "typical" system weighs in at 16 pounds—light enough to be considered transportable but probably not portable.

SOFTWARE

"Software" is simply another word for programs. Without a program or set of instructions to follow, computers would not be very smart. The IBM PC family of products has a wide variety of very good software available. However, the PCjr™ has a few idiosyncracies that make some care mecessary when selecting your software.

The major consideration is the amount of RAM required to run the program. The PC and XT can be configured to handle 256K of on-board memory and up to 896K with the aid of expansion boards; the PCjr™ has a maximum physical capacity of 128K. This memory restriction can either rule out a given program, or, at the least, limit its performance. This limitation can become all too brutally apparent when, after spending hours at the office inputting data to a program that uses a 256K memory, you discover you are unable to access files on your home PCjr™.

Another consideration is that the PCjr™ has but one disk drive. In some applications, particularly spreadsheets, one disk drive is dedicated to act as a program drive, and a second drive must be used to access the data files.

Software offerings for the PCjr™ include special versions of EasyWriter™, Time Manager™, pfs:FILE™, pfs:REPORT™, BASIC Programming Development System™, Casino Games™, Strategy Games™, and Logo™. Some of the new software packages that are available for the PCjr™ are Monster Math™, Animation Creation™, Mouser™, Scuba Venture™, Homeword™, Crossfire™, Mine Shaft™, Bumble Games™, Juggles' Butterfly™, Turtle Power™, Adventures in Math™, Home Budget jr™, and Personal Communications Manager™.

The software that seems to have the greatest reliance on the cartridge slot arrangement is BASIC itself. Cassette BASIC is resident in system ROM and always there to provide display support, primary logic, and math functions; however the 32K of cartridge BASIC, which uses the cartridge slot, must be in place before the computer will even allow you to load a BASIC language extentions. Further, the Graphics Macro Language™ and Music Macro Language™, two special functions that control the computer's ability to display its special graphics and sound features, are on this same cartridge.

The following software is known not to run on the PCjr™: DOS 1.1 and 2.0, Asynchronous Communications 2.0, BASIC Primer 1.0, Binary Synchronous 3270 Emulation™, BPI Accounting™, BASIC Compiler™, Decathlon™, Fact Track™, FORTRAN™, Learning DOS™, Learning to Program in BASIC™, VisiCalc™ 1.0 and 1.1, Mailing List Manager™, Peachtree Accounting Software, Private Tutor™, 3101 Emulation, Typing Tutor™, and the UCSD p-System™.

Table 1-2 Versions of PC-DOS

DOS VERSION	PC*jr*™	IBM PC	IBM XT
DOS 2.1	yes	yes	yes
DOS 2.0	no	yes	yes
DOS 1.1	no	yes	no

There is also a classification of PC software that in some case requires the PC*jr*™ DOS (or the version of DOS in the program disk) to be modified or, in other cases, there are special considerations necessary to use them. Among these are: Arithmetic Games™, Multiplan™, Multiplication Tables™, Peachtext™, Personal Editor™, Basic Compiler™, Diskette Librarian™, Dow Jones Reporter™, Easywriter™ 1.10, Learning DOS™ 2.0 version 1.0, Learning to Program in Basic™, Logo™ 1.0, Mailing List Manager™ 1.0, Private Tutor™ 1.0, Professional Editor™ 1.0, Visicalc™ 1.2, and Word Proof™ 1.0.

In most cases the necessary steps to run these programs are very simple, but they must be done by the user. For our purposes here, suffice it to say that these programs can be operated, but only with certain conditions. For additional information, refer to Chapter 11.

PC*jr*™ OVERVIEW

This chapter gave you a general overview of the PC*jr*™ and some of it's capabilities. The PC*jr*™ brings a lot of muscle to the world of home computers. It is, really, a series of systems designed for both home and limited office use. It can start out as a simple, yet exciting, home-game system and be built into a very powerful little computer. As we continue our exploration of this latest addition to the IBM family of products, you will discover more about its design, functionality, usefulness, and other attributes will in all likelihood make the PC*jr*™ one of the most popular microcomputers on the market.

So to answer the question posed at the beginning of this chapter, "Yes we do need another home computer, and the PC*jr*™ is it!"

CHAPTER 2

PUTTING JUNIOR TO WORK

GETTING READY

In the previous chapter, you learned exactly what equipment is available for the PCJr and the various ways you might buy it. This chapter shows you some of the ways you can use this handy, inexpensive computer in the home, office, or school, or as a substitute for the larger PC you use in the office. Specifically, we will look at the two models, entry level and enhanced version, and we will explain how to add features to the enhanced model to increase its usefulness even further.

As we have said, the PC*jr*™ is a versatile product capable of performing a wide range of applications and tasks. In the home, you might use it to keep track of the membership of your local club or PTA. You wouldn't need the enhanced model to do this; the entry level can handle such tasks, although storing information onto a cassette will be more time consuming. But it is the enhanced model that is intended to provide compatibility with the larger PC, thus allowing you to swap programs and data between machines by simply exchanging diskettes.

If you choose to upgrade the enhanced model you can add significantly to its capability. For example, by adding the integrated modem, you are able to access outside data bases such as the Dow Jones stock market quotations. And if you have a similar modem on the PC in your office you can access its files from your home. Under some circumstances and with authorized log-in procedures you can even work with information which resides on your corporate computer.

Whether or not you are able to create a direct link from home to office, with the necessary word-processing software, you will be able to produce letters, reports, and memoranda at home. Such documents can be enhanced with business graphics to make your presentation more forceful. All you need is an appropriate graphics package.

The key to your satisfaction with the PC*jr*™ lies in tying together two bodies of knowledge: what it is that you want to accomplish and what programs or hardware enhancements are required to facilitate these tasks.

PUTTING IT TOGETHER

Are you worried about how to get your computer up and running? This may prove to be a lot easier than you think. The IBM people have so configured the hardware that all you need do is to follow a few simple directions.

The entry level model consists of the system unit, keyboard, adapter cable to match the system to the desired display, plus the power supply.

Connecting these devices is simple. Find the power supply, really an AC adaptor designed to give the system proper power and to avoid transients (voltage spikes), and the connector called *power* located on the right side of the rear panel. But wait, don't connect them just yet.

Next, turn the keyboard over and place four AA 1.5V batteries in the compartment designated for them. Restrain your eagerness to start it up; don't turn on the keyboard just yet either.

Now, we'll assume that you are using a television for the display. Connect the special television adapter cable to the input leads of the television. This doesn't mean that you have to disconnect the TV from its customary antenna or electrical outlet. It will continue to draw its electricity from its own electric cord and, if you'd like, you can keep the TV set connected to the antenna. Just be sure to turn the adapter switch to make the connection to the computer when you want to use it for your video screen display.

But, as you must certainly have been told, you aren't required to use your television set for this purpose. Any relatively inexpensive monitor will work just as well if it can handle a composite video signal. We recommend that you purchase one of several offered today that include a built-in sound amplifier and speaker. You will get a better image and avoid quarrels with members of your family on who gets access to the family TV.

A switch on the TV connector module toggles between the TV and computer settings in order to keep your PC*jr*™ off the air.

Once you have the system connected correctly, go ahead and plug in the power supply. Don't worry that the keyboard isn't connected to anything. It isn't supposed to be. Then turn the keyboard on, locating it in front of the system unit. It will work within a 60-degree angle to either side as well as above or below the system unit and the same angle with respect to the position of the keyboard's vertical relationship to the system unit. But for now keep things lined up until you are more familiar with what to expect.

Now turn on the computer as well. The first thing the PC*jr*™ is going to do is run a power-on self-test to verify that it is able to operate properly. The first picture you will see on your color TV screen is the IBM logo with 16 color bars.

While the system is checking itself out, this display will stay in view. It only takes a few seconds—but a little longer is required if you have the enhanced unit, since there is more memory and more, therefore, to verify.

Once the PC*jr*™ is satisfied that everything is working in a proper manner, it will sound a beep to indicate everything is OK. Then it will clear the screen and load BASIC version 1.1. This may surprise you, for there is no need to mount a cartridge or use a cassette or disk drive in order to "come up" in BASIC. While this version of BASIC is called Cassette BASIC it is nevertheless resident in the ROM (Read Only Memory) of the machine.

What happens next depends on the system you have purchased and how it is configured. With the entry level system, you must tell the system that you want to load an application. But with the enhanced, disk-equipped system, an application will automatically load.

But the same is true with the basic system if you already have installed a cartridge in one of the two slots. The PC*jr*™ automatically queries these slots to see what's there. If either a disk or cartridge is available, the PC*jr*™ will "read" what is stored on it.

But since this is the first time through, you might want to find out more about the keyboard. Therefore, whether or not there is a disk or cartridge ready to run something else, depress the ESCape key in the upper left-hand corner of the keyboard. The PC*jr*™ will then load a program called "Keyboard Adventure." Like BASIC, it too is stored in ROM.

You will probably find this an exciting exercise, and any time you want to learn more about the keyboard, you can go through the course of instruction it provides. If you get tired of it, simply depress the ESCape and ALT keys. This will bring you back to BASIC.

We know that you are interested in the operation of the PC*jr*™ keyboard. It is somewhat different from other keyboards presently on the market, and because it is, we've devoted the whole of Chapter 3 and Appendix A to it.

Many of the programs you can buy come with keyboard overlays to enable you to use the keyboard correctly for a particular purpose or application. And for those programs that you may write yourself, you can devise your own overlays. It's not a bad idea, and it makes your machine a great deal more flexible.

LET'S TALK BASIC

Once the machine is ready to go, you're already in the BASIC language. IBM has gone to a lot of trouble to make this BASIC easy to use and expandable. The BASIC that you use in the entry level machine is known as Cassette BASIC. By itself, as you will see, it is pretty powerful. However, you can make it more powerful by adding Cartridge BASIC, which can also be used for disk operation as well.

To avoid re-entering your programs by typing them each time, you will probably want to add a tape recorder. We suggest that you buy one that is well made and easy to use. A number of good ones are available that fit on the desk top and take a standard-sized tape. The one shown in Fig. 2-1 lets you slip the tape cartridge in from the top via a pop-up lid. It has a built-in tape counter, which is important since it helps you to locate the programs on the tape. IBM does not offer a cassette recorder unit as part of the package, either with the entry level device or with the enhanced version. However, IBM does offer a connecting cable.

As shown in Fig. 2-2, the tape unit has connectors for an earphone, microphone, and remote control. Your recorder may be slightly different

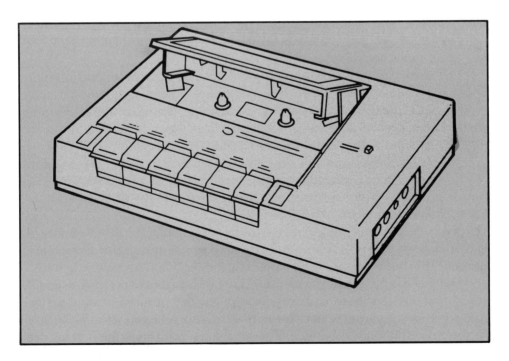

Fig. 2-1.   **Typical cassette recorder.**

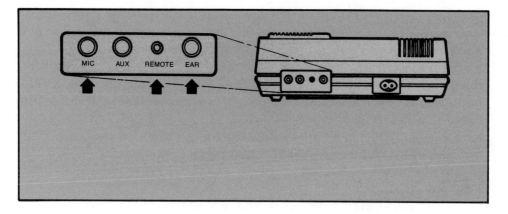

Fig. 2-2. **Connectors for microphone, earphone, and remote control.**

from the one we are showing, but it should have all the same connectors even if they are named somewhat differently. If your recorder has an AUX, or auxiliary connector, ignore it. PC*jr*™ will work just fine with the microphone connector. However, you need a cable to connect the PC*jr*™ to the recorder. We think it's best to buy the cable from IBM when you purchase your system. The PC*jr*™ can now use the cassette recorder to load and save programs. We'll show you how shortly.

If you have purchased your cable from IBM, you will note that there is a special connector on one end called a DIN plug. This connector has a special notch at the top to make sure it plugs in correctly—they thought of everything.

SAVING THE PROGRAM

When you want to load or save a program in Cassette BASIC all you do is type the word "SAVE." Since the tape unit is the only device recognized by Cassette BASIC, the output will be directed to the cassette port.

This tape cassette device serves as a data recorder. It is used to save and load BASIC programs or text data files. You can use just about any recorder you want with the system, but we recommend one of good quality. Almost all such tape recording units operate both from batteries and from house current. Just to ensure things go right at the beginning, you might start by using house current. The reason for this is that the receiver on the computer side expects data at a certain level, at a certain speed. So far as "volume control" is concerned, about mid-range on most recorders works quite well. But if the batteries are low, the rate of transfer will slow down and the computer won't recognize the information. Then you will get a "load error."

With everything set up, put a new cassette in the recorder. If the cassette has a leader (a clear piece of tape) let the recorder run past this or the data won't record correctly. You may have to unplug the remote control cable to let the recorder run. Once you're past the leader—and you can avoid this nuisance by buying tape designed for transcription—plug the remote cable back in if necessary, depress the proper buttons so that you are now in "record," and turn your PC*jr*™ on.

Once the PC*jr*™ gets into BASIC, type in the following program. Don't worry what the codes mean. What they do will become evident shortly.

```
10   CLS
20   PRINT "THE CASSETTE WORKS"
30   FOR I = 1 TO 1000
40   PRINT I;
50   NEXT I
60   CLS
70   END
```

With this on your screen, your cursor—the little block that moves as you type—should be right below the 70. You are now ready to save the program. But before doing so, make sure that the recorder is, in fact, in the record mode.

Ready? Then type the following: SAVE "CAS1:TEST1".

You could have omitted the CAS1: since the PC*jr*™ knows that only one device can be used with Cassette BASIC. Now depress the Enter key. If you look at the recorder, the spindles should be moving, showing that data is being recorded. Once the program is recorded, BASIC will respond with an Ok. This tells you that it got everything and is ready to do business again.

Since we are going to test this out, you probably want to have an idea of how everything should work. First type LIST and depress the Enter key. Now the program that you just entered and saved should list itself out on the screen.

Try typing a "RUN" to see what happens. Just type RUN and depress the Enter key again. The screen will clear, the PC*jr*™ will print one line of text and will then count to 1000. Then the screen will clear again, and the Ok prompt will appear in the upper left-hand corner. That shows you that so far everything is in order and the system is working the way it is supposed to. At the same time it demonstrates one of the functions a computer does well: count.

Now type the word LIST again. This will show you that the program you have entered is not only on tape but is also still in the computer's memory.

Every time you type RUN it will do the same thing it did before. But that isn't what we want to do at the moment.

With the program listed on your screen, type the word NEW and depress the Enter key. NEW is a special word in BASIC that causes the program currently in memory to be erased. (Don't worry about it. The program is still stored on your tape cassette.) To prove this to yourself, type CLS (to *clear* the *screen*). Then depress Enter. This will, of course, clear the screen, (another important word in BASIC). Then type LIST again and depress the Enter key. Notice nothing is listed because you erased the program with NEW.

Now to get the program back from the tape. Believe it or not, this is easy to do. All we have to do is LOAD it. Remember that after we recorded the program we didn't do anything with the recorder. Therefore, the tape is past where the program is recorded, so it's necessary to rewind the tape. In order to do this, you might depress the Stop button and remove the remote control cable in order to put the recorder in rewind, but it happens that the PC*jr*™ can do part of the work for you and makes it possible for you to avoid plugging and unplugging the remote cable.

All that is necessary is to put the recorder in the proper mode of operation. In this case, depress the Rewind button. Don't touch the cables. Now on the keyboard, type, MOTOR 1 and depress the Enter key. The recorder will go into the rewind mode. "MOTOR" is another function which has been built into the PC*jr*™'s BASIC language.

Now you need to tell the recorder to stop once the tape is rewound. To do this, type, MOTOR 0 and depress the Enter key. The motor will stop and you can set up for the next mode. Now depress the Play button on the recorder.

Type on the keyboard, LOAD "CAS1:TEST1" and depress the Enter key. Just as when you were saving the program, the recorder will begin running and when the load is complete, you will get an Ok on the screen. If you type LIST, the program will list out the same instructions you typed in and reviewed before. Of course a RUN will cause it to execute just as it did before.

There are variations to what we have done. You could have had the program begin to run as soon as it was loaded by simply typing, LOAD "CAS1:TEST1",R. (Note that in this case the "R" means to run.) In addition, you could have left off the CAS1: since Cassette BASIC will look for the program only on the tape recorder. You could have just typed LOAD and depressed Enter. This causes the first program available on the tape to be loaded, and since only one program presently exists and you are at the start of the tape, it would have loaded TEST1.

However, if you had not rewound the tape or if it was unable to load properly, you would have received an error message: "DEVICE TIMEOUT", or "PROGRAM NOT FOUND". The first error is reported when the PC*jr*™ isn't getting the proper signals. The second is reported when it can't find the right name on the cassette. If, while searching for a program with a given name, the search goes past some other program or data file name, it will tell you the name of the file or program that was skipped.

If you're planning on using the PC*jr*™ with the cassette system, here are a few additional words of advice. First, buy only good cassettes. Try to choose only high-quality, high-bias tapes. The less costly tapes can give you a lot of trouble that even PC*jr*™ can't compensate for. Second, be sure to follow the instructions on the tape for taking care of them. After all you just may put the one important program on it that you can't live without.

In addition, observe the following rules:

- Never touch the magnetic surface of the tape. Handle the tapes by the plastic case only.
- Always insert the tape in the recorder with the magnetic surface facing the proper direction.
- Never force the tape in— you may break the recorder.
- Be sure that the tape is tightly wound. If it is loose, it may catch in the pinch rollers either breaking or damaging the data on it.
- Write protect tapes by breaking out the small tab at the back after you have saved your program or data. If you need to write on a tape after you have write-protected it, a piece of Scotch tape where the tab was will restore the "write" function.
- Be sure to clean your tape recorder heads. If you use the recorder a lot, this becomes important since oxides can build up and eventually cause damage to the tape.

Cassette BASIC is a minimal BASIC, but, as we've shown you, it can do a lot of things, such as support a light pen, joysticks, address the printer, and let you edit lines of program code.

MORE IS ADDED WITH CARTRIDGE BASIC

You should now have a pretty good idea of what you can do with Cassette BASIC and the entry level system. Now you might be interested in some of the things you can add that will enhance your PC*jr*™.

For starters, you can begin by purchasing Cartridge BASIC. This is an enhanced version of the language that uses some of the capabilities already found in the ROMs in Cassette BASIC. In addition, Cartridge BASIC is designed to work with the disk operating system.

If you aren't using the disk system, getting into Cartridge BASIC is as simple as inserting the cartridge in the left cartridge slot (Fig. 2-3). You'll use the other slot for any games or other software that require BASIC.

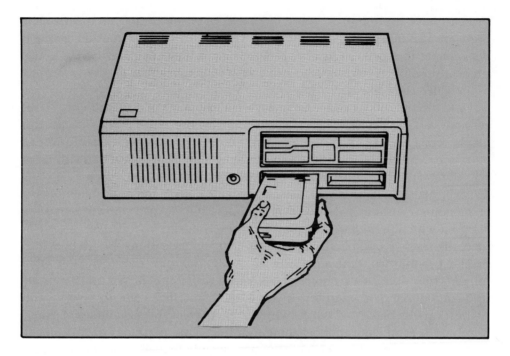

Fig. 2-3. **ROM cartridge being plugged into cartridge slot.**

We've reserved Chapter 5 for showing you how to use Cartridge BASIC. You might want to skip to that chapter to get an idea of what we have in mind. But if you're interested in the display card and disk drive, read on.

BOOSTING THE MEMORY AND DISPLAY

As you already know, the entry level system is restricted to 40 columns of display because of the limitations of the home television set. The restriction on how much "information" you can describe or display in a given area is due to limited bandwidth. In the case of television, there is a minimal area to work with, so in order to get words and graphics to come out legible and undistorted, you stay within 40 columns.

Although a standard television display works fine for some computer applications, it is not ideal for the display of text or intricate graphic designs. For these purposes, it is best to have a display system that doesn't blank every other line, a *non-interlaced display*. Such a display is capable of showing the maximum amount of information possible. The ideal is 1000 lines by 1000 rows, and some very costly displays can do this.

The PC*jr*™, however, doesn't do badly. For example, with the enhanced version, or with the optional display card mounted in the entry-level version, you can have up to 640 × 200 dots of screen resolution. This means that there are 128,000 possible locations on which a unit of information (a single dot—sometimes called a pixel or picture element) can be placed. This is the highest possible resolution you can have, and it requires all the resources of the video RAM to handle it.

On the enhanced version, or with the display card in the entry-level version, you can display four different colors at the same time. Without the display card you are only allowed four colors at the medium resolution of 320 × 200 pixels. With the card in medium resolution mode you can have 16 colors. The entry unit is the only one that provides low resolution (160 × 200) mode. Of course you may have to fiddle with the available monitor or TV adjustments in order to get the proper shades, and you will also need a screen which provides good quality representation. The display card does more than add 16,000-plus additional video memory locations. Beside boosting display capabilities, it also permits the use of a better, more "capable" terminal. Thus, you have a choice of black and white or color, or an IBM or an IBM-compatible color monitor. If you wish to sacrifice color in favor of the highest quality black and white (which depicts color only as shades of gray), purchase a composite monochrome monitor. This is preferable to color if your major concern is to obtain the most legible display of text characters for word processing and the general treatment of text files.

The special card you would purchase for the display of color also provides you with another 64K bytes of RAM to add to your system. This brings the total memory to 128K. Moreover, with that much memory you can add a disk drive for the random access storage and retrieval of files and further increase the system's capability.

THE SOUNDS OF MUSIC

As we've explained earlier and will expand upon in Chapter 10, the PCjr™ has the ability to generate three levels of sound with three different "voices." This is accomplished with a Texas Instruments SN76496N complex sound generator. Since it is a port-located device you can poke information to it to create complex sounds.

THE DISK STORES MORE

The most important add-on for the PCjr™ is the disk system, a 5¼-inch low-profile drive that can store up to 360,000 pieces (bytes) of information. Part of this storage is taken up with a portion of the operating system, called

PC-DOS 2.1. If you're familiar with PC-DOS, you have a working knowledge of DOS 2.1, which is different from 2.0, as discussed in Chapter 6.

If you already have a PC or XT and are interested in getting an idea of how DOS 2.1 differs from 2.0, you can change the disk base parameter of your 2.0 version (located at 78 Hex) to the following:

DB 11001111B, 3, 25H,2,8, 2AH, 0FFH, 50H, 0F6H, 25, 4

This will cause DOS 2.0 to respond to the slower 6 millisecond track-to-track access time found on the PC*jr*™. IBM offers a maintenance diskette that upgrades 2.0 to match 2.1 for those of you who already have a PC or XT.

INSTALLING A DISK

To install the necessary disk controller board, lift up the top of the PC system unit, plug the "adapter" board into the slot provided and mount the "disk drive." Unlike the PC or XT, only one drive is currently supported. Since the important input/output functions of DOS are contained in the system ROM, you need only boot or load DOS once; then you can change to another diskette of your choice for whatever programs you want to run. You can use the cassette recorder as an auxiliary device as well.

The operation of the disk drive is interesting in itself. If you're unfamiliar with the operation of a disk storage unit, it is well worth studying. Whole books have been written on the operation. We do not intend to write a book on disk drives, but we would like to provide some information to assist you in understanding the actual operation.

A disk drive is nothing but a high-performance record player. The differences are that the tracks aren't spiral but concentric (Fig. 2-4) and that the information is stored in a digital rather than analog form, which means it is either signal or no-signal rather than a range of signals of varying frequencies or intensities. Further, each track is divided into sectors (Fig. 2-5). For the PC*jr*™ and other IBM PCs the sectors are 512 bytes in length, and there are nine sectors of 512 bytes within each of 40 usable tracks per diskette surface. Since the PC*jr*™'s diskette is double-sided, it has 80 usable tracks and thus 360K bytes of storage capacity. The drive operates at 300 rpm, which allows data to come off at 250,000 bits per second.

The disk system is made up of drive mechanics, diskette, a read/write head, and the necessary electronics to make it work. All of this is bundled into a system with a controller so that the unit can talk to the PC*jr*™.

The disk system is useless, however, without the driving software called the operating system. This software matches the performance and hardware

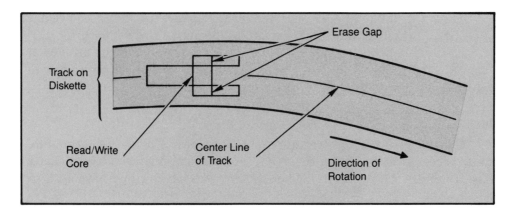

Fig. 2-4. **Diskette tracks.**

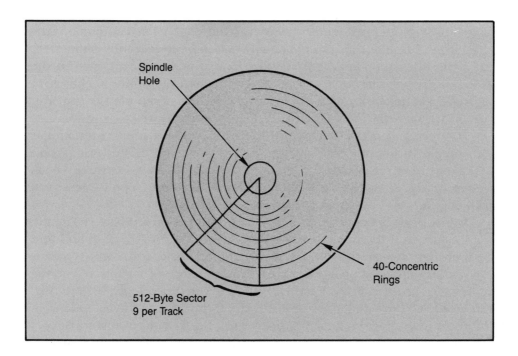

Fig. 2-5. **Diskette sectors.**

design of the disk drive and remembers what goes where when. For example, if you ask for the file called "inventory" the operating system finds it in a directory which also keeps information on the track and sector where the data can be found.

Once the location is known, a signal called a "seek" is issued and the disk drive head is moved in or out to the approprate track. In addition, the proper header is sought as the sectors rotate under the head. All of this takes time, which is referred to as the "latency" of the drive. It can take as long as 8.3 milliseconds. Added to the track-to-track access time of 6 milliseconds, it amounts to a long time to find the data when compared to a larger system with a speedier drive. Nonetheless, this technique of data access is much faster than using a cassette or finding it in a file drawer by hand.

The overall result of all these manipulations is that you see data appear either on the CRT screen, on the printer, or possibly written out to the cassette drive.

Like the larger PCs, the disk system will try to boot on powering up the system. You can get directly to Cassette or Cartridge BASIC, however, simply by depressing the CONtrol and ESCape keys together, even if you did boot up the disk system.

If you need to reset the system, you can do so by performing a "CTRL-ALT-DEL" key sequence. (This means pressing the Control, Alternate, and Delete keys simultaneously.) As with the larger PCs, this causes a software reset and reboots the disk drive. Those of you who are familiar with the regular PC and the XT models will recognize that there is a great deal of similarity.

STILL MORE IS ADDED

There is still more that can be added to the PCjr™, such as joysticks, a parallel or serial printer, a modem and a light pen. The light pen, which plugs into the rear panel, is not only supported by the hardware, but all the versions of BASIC make provisions for its use. The chapter on BASIC will give you some idea of how to use the light pen in application programs. Later we'll give you an idea of how it can be used with commercial applications as well.

CHAPTER 3

THE MAGIC KEYBOARD

MORE THAN A KEYBOARD

A computer keyboard usually isn't thought of as anything very special. That is unless it is cordless, communicates with the computer console by light waves, is fully programmable, and for all practical purposes, is a micro-computer itself. And that, of course, is precisely what the PC*jr*™'s keyboard does and is. Let's begin our analysis of the keyboard by looking at its external characteristics. This, after all, is what you will be looking at and working with.

The keyboard, shown in Fig 3-1, is a detached, extremely portable, battery operated unit (uses four AA-sized 1.5 volt batteries). An optional six-foot keyboard cable does allow operating the keyboard without batteries through a direct connection to the back panel of the system unit. It is smaller in size than most—measuring 13.45 × 6.61 × 1.02 inches. It weighs in at an incredible 25 ounces!

Fig. 3-1.   PC*jr*™'s wireless keyboard.

Packed into this small real estate, are 62 keys that use full travel, **carbon** contact/rubber dome technology. That means they offer the normal stroke length, derive their spring or resistance from the use of rubber dome-shaped supports that lie underneath the keycaps, and make their electrical contacts by means of carbon points.

The keys are arranged in a standard typewriter layout, with the addition of a special function key FN and cursor control keys. The keyboard has special color coding to identify special functions.

One thing that you may have noticed is that the key tops aren't labeled. The tags or identifiers for each key are printed above it. In many cases there is more than one meaning, as you will gather from examining Fig. 3-2.

The keyboard also contains a special serial port that can either be connected to the system unit via the cable, or it can communicate with the system unit via infrared light that is modulated and encoded for each key stroke.

The infrared data link is one of the most unique features of this keyboard, there is none other like it. This technology is explained further in Appendix A. The use of a wireless connection gives greater flexibility in the positioning of the keyboard and eliminates the cumbersome interface cable.

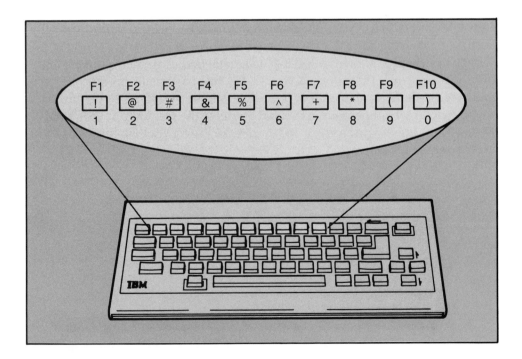

Fig. 3-2.   **Many of PC*jr*™'s keys have multiple meanings.**

Wireless operation is limited to a range of about 20 feet and requires line-of-site access. The keyboard does have to be "pointed" toward the system unit, however, the pointing is not critical since the infrared signal radiates with approximately a 60-degree angle. You can move within the 60-degree angle, side-to-side, or up and down in relationship to the system unit. Thus you can place your PCjr™ at a convenient location, such as on your stereo cabinet, and move yourself and keyboard about the room for your convenience. (Fig. 3-3)

In order to provide greater ease in typing, you may raise or lower the angle of the keyboard. Some people like it to sit fairly flat on their desk. Others prefer it to be slanted somewhat. Feet on the bottom can be adjusted to satisfy your particular preferences in relation to the surface where you position it. You can vary the angle selecting either five or twelve degree tilt. You may be wondering whether or not the keyboard will interfere with the infrared remote control on your television, video tape recorder or disk player, or whether it, in turn, might interfere with them. The answer is probably not. As you will find in Appendix A, infrared devices use a special coding scheme to send information. In this fashion interference is minimized from dissimilar devices. IBM admits that it is "possible, though unlikely" that the keyboard could use the same frequency as some other household electronics products, with a resulting potential for interference if both are used simultaneously.

Certainly, you can get interference from another PCjr™'s keyboard since your system would recognize it as a valid device. Therefore, IBM recommends that when more than one PCjr™ is being used within the same room the optional keyboard cable be attached. When this cable is used to establish the serial link, the infrared and battery circuitry are disabled and the system unit provides power.

You may choose to ignore this advice under certain circumstances. An interesting aspect of the infra-red keyboard is that you can create multiple-player interactive games. Thus several players could play the game, each with his or her own keyboard. Also think of the possibility of tutoring with several keyboards, an instructor and several students could access the PCjr™ and use it as a learning tool. Although this is possible, there are some difficulties that you will have to be aware of.

First, the infrared link is a serial link. This means that it expects data to flow to it one bit at a time. Moreover, it can handle only one device at a time. Interference may occur if more than one device tries to send data to the system at the same time. The keystrokes from the various keyboards may get intermixed or garbled or possibly not recognized at all. However, by coordinating the use of the keyboards all could communicate with one PCjr™ interactively.

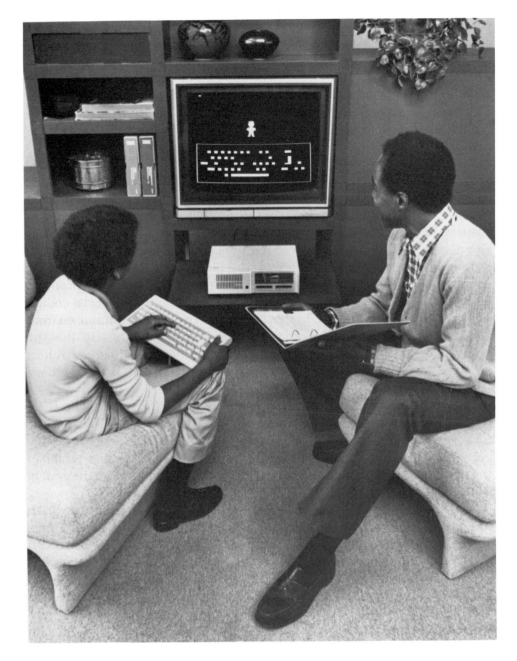

Fig. 3-3.　Conveniently placed PC*jr*™ and detached keyboard.

VERY SMART INDEED

As we indicated at the beginning, the PCjr™ keyboard has only 62-keys. This may not seem like very many, especially when you consider that the PC and XT have 83-keys. To see the differences, take a look at Figs. 3-4 and 3-5. Here we have compared the PC/XT keyboard with PCjr™'s . Notice that some PC/XT keys are missing. For example, the Function keys are now located along the top and also serve as the numeric keys. The function key codes are generated in conjunction with the ALT key and the function key. This does not interfere with the normal "upshift" use of the same key. The keyboard can generate 256 individual codes depending on how the combinations of CONTROL, ALT, FN and SHIFT are used. In addition, the special function key FN, located to the upper right, is used in conjunction with other keys—such as Q for "pause" and P for "print screen." You can also use this key for special purposes when you write your own programs.

Can the keyboard keep up with your typing speed? Indeed yes. It can buffer up to sixteen keystrokes at a time. Thus you're able to stay ahead of the system unit and keep the infrared link full of data.

Looking below the surface. The keyboard relies on an 80C48 Intel microprocessor and a series of quad latches to handle the signals from the key switches. In addition, the keyboard could be augmented with 16K bytes of internal CMOS RAM. What this would mean and what it would accomplish is not yet clear from IBM's documentation. We will await with interest future announcements to see what the company may have up its sleeve.

This additional RAM could mean that you could establish a series of keystrokes that are switched in and out via single keystroke. Thus we could end up with a "hidden" keyboard full of programmable functions.

If you get into programming you may want the program to be on the lookout for specific codes. With the BASIC language you do have available a way to test these codes using the CHR$ function. A little later we'll show you how to set up your keyboard for special applications.

IT WORKS BY SYMMETRY

The keyboard can be thought of as a matrix of horizontal and vertical wires that are intersected by key switches. The keyboard decoder/encoder circuitry generates keyboard scan codes and the key switches generate a return signal. Both lines are pulled high until a key is depressed. At that time both lines become one and a key closure at a matrix junction is sensed. Essentially, the matrix is a series of open circuits with a watchdog waiting for a key to close.

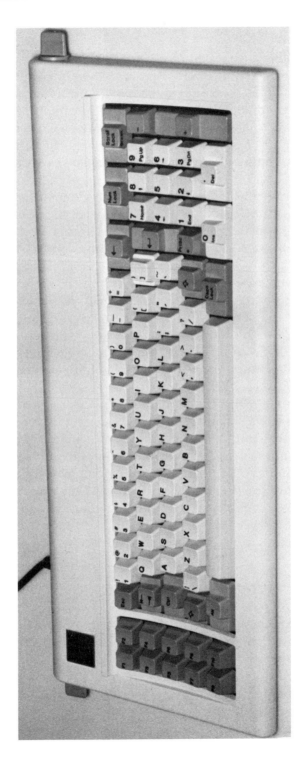

Fig. 3-4.   Standard IBM PC keyboard.

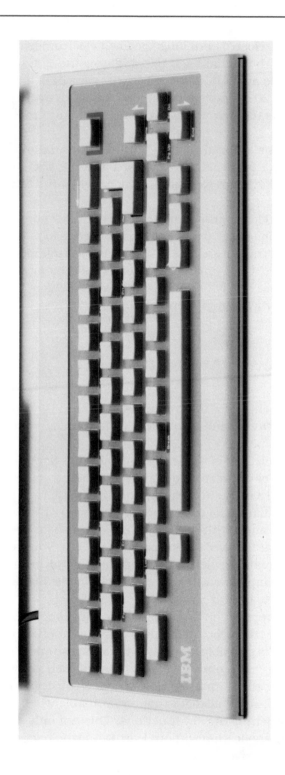

Fig. 3-5. PCjr™ keyboard.

When the key is closed, both lines "go low," electronically speaking, and an inverter brings the signal back to a high on the 80C48 databus. The typical signal time is about 440 microseconds, thus data is sent at a rate of 1200 baud (about 120 characters per second) between the keyboard and the system unit. Time is required though for the system unit to look at the data, and verify it.

When used in the infrared mode, additional information is added by the keyboard to indicate that this is a keyboard and not something else. This code comes from a keyboard ROM and is added when the infrared circuit is enabled—otherwise it is ignored.

Unlike standard keyboards that expect at the most only one or two keys to be depressed, PC*jr*™ can sense the closure of several keys at once, to create a modified output. This means that the data is multiplexed—combined on the data bus of the 80C48 microprocessor. This data is compared to the character ROM to see if it is valid and either a correct key signal is sent on or an error signal or warning is generated.

CREATE YOUR OWN KEYBOARD

The flexibility behind the electronic design of the PC*jr*™ keyboard makes it possible for you to redefine it to "build" one to meet your own needs or specifications.

Currently, the method of doing this is to assign certain keys to perform special functions. For example, you may decide that it would be desirable to have F10 always call a menu in the program. Therefore, your program would look for the generation of the code represented by an ALT 0.

The way you would set the keyboard up is to use an overlay. This is a cardboard mask that fits over the keyboard (Fig. 3-6). You can write or type on these cards to create the desired arrangement. It seems as if it would be easier to create a template on the computer, fill in the blanks and dump it to the printer than to do this by hand.

An interesting application would be to turn the keyboard into something that would resemble the keyboard of a piano, or would serve the same general purpose. Actually it is probably more like a music synthesizer keyboard since you have to use more than one row. You can mark each key with the appropriate note, and use the sound function to create the desired note.

Many of the software packages that are available will come with a keyboard overlay to indentify the key functions. This not only allows you to get the most out of the application without learning a whole set of special codes,

Fig. 3-6.   **Keyboard and overlay.**

but makes you more productive in the process. Generally speaking, you can make the keyboard work the way you want it to.

In most cases you will find that definitions for keys that work with the PC/XT will also work with the PC*jr*™. However, it is critical that you do make the notation on the overlay.

CHAPTER 4

THE DISPLAY SYSTEM

Now that you know how to talk to the computer, you need to understand how the computer talks to you. One of the ways in which it does this is to display information on a monitor or television. Whichever model of the PC*jr*™ you purchase, you need a way of displaying its information on a screen.

The PC*jr*™ is designed to be used with three different display systems: a home color television, an IBM color monitor, or a composite video display. Each display system offers you somewhat different capabilities. The question is, which one is for you? This chapter describes in detail the operation of the various display systems. You will be shown what you need to make each one work and what programs will operate with what display device. In addition, you will be shown how each device is correctly connected to the PC*jr*™.

HOME COLOR TV

Before we look at which monitor is best for which application, let's make sure that we all understand the differences between the types of monitors. Probably the most popular monitor used with the PC*jr*™ is the home color television. It is the one monitor that all of us already have. Purchasing a monitor can add from a few hundred to six hundred or more dollars to the cost of the system. Since the PC*jr*™ will quickly become a member of the family (Fig. 4-1), it will usually be placed near the family TV anyway, so why not make use of it?

How does the computer send signals to a TV and how does the TV understand them? They are not the normal signals received from the antenna; instead they are just a stream of meaningless data. What causes the TV to recognize this data and convert it to a usable display on the family TV set?

Fig. 4-1.   **A typical installation of the PC*jr*™
using the family color TV as a monitor.**

This is done through a converter that is optionally available with the
PC*jr*™. This converter takes the data output from the computer and converts
it to energy the TV recognizes as normal television signals. If we think of the
converter as a miniature, very low-powered TV station, it will be easier to
grasp this concept. The computer outputs its data into the converter, which
translates it into both video (picture) and sound information. It then trans-
mits this information on a frequency (channel) that the TV recognizes as a
standard TV signal. The TV does not know that it is receiving anything other
than a standard TV signal, so it obligingly displays it on the screen and
sends the audio portion of the signal to its amplifier and speaker system.

If you connected the converter to an antenna instead of directly to the
TV set, the signal would radiate into the air and still be received by the TV.
Since the converter is such a low-powered transmitter, the range of your
own private TV station would be extremely limited. Even so, do not try this.
The Federal Communications Commission [FCC] do not appreciate unau-
thorized transmission, and they do not have a sense of humor.

Note that the converter device meets all of the FCC rules and regulations when connected *exactly as described* in the IBM PCjr™ instruction manuals.

THE IBM COLOR MONITOR

The next form of display supported by the PCjr™ is the existing IBM color monitor. The same monitor is sold for use with the PCjr™'s big brothers, the PC and XT computers. A *dedicated* monitor such as this differs from a television in two important ways: it does not have a tuner that selects a channel, and it requires direct coupled video instead of a transmitted signal.

One advantage of this type of display over a standard TV set is that it is specifically designed to accept input directly from the computer, so its electronic circuits are matched to the output from the computer. A second advantage is that the signal it receives from the computer is divided into video and the three primary colors, red, green, and blue (hence the term RGB monitor).

Information displayed on this type of monitor will be of better quality than that shown on a standard TV for two reasons: first, the information received from the computer is fed directly into the video section of the monitor without undergoing a series of conversions, and second, since the sole function of the monitor is to display computer data, it has been specially designed to permit a higher quality image to be displayed on the screen.

COMPOSITE VIDEO MONITOR

A composite video monitor has also been specially designed to receive information directly from the computer, but in this case all of the information is combined on a single wire. The computer mixes the information required to create a signal that is composed of the characters and the colors, and sends it out to the monitor. The resolution or quality of the displayed image is better than that displayed on a TV set, but not quite a good as that of the RGB monitor.

WHICH MONITOR IS FOR YOU?

To properly evaluate the types of display modes supported by the PCjr we should discuss the two separate models of the system. The entry level model provides color graphics output for either of the two color devices listed above, but in the text mode, the system is limited to 40 columns by 25 lines. This may or may not be a limitation, depending upon the software applications of the user.

A 40 column display is useful for many of the home and educational software programs available for the PC*jr*, but for work with business or home accounting software, word processing, or spreadsheets, a full 80 column display is preferable. The reason that the entry mode is provided with 40 columns rather than 80 is the limitation placed on the system by the use of a TV as a monitor. Televisions do not have the bandwidth to display a full 80 columns across the screen. The characters become distorted and even totally unreadable at the sides of the screen.

In order to display a full 80 columns of text, it is necessary either to purchase the upgrade from the entry level system to the enhanced system or to purchase the enhanced system from the start.

But even the enhanced version involves some tradeoffs in displaying the computer's output. If you want to utilize the graphics capabilities of the system and still have the ability to display word processing and spreadsheets in the 80-column format, you may still have to make some compromises. We will delve more deeply into these tradeoffs later in this chapter. For now the reader need only recognize that there are at least three different variations of display output provided by the PC*jr*™.

ENTRY MODEL DISPLAY

Since the entry level system mainly used in education and games, the first choice in a monitor will most likely be the user's own color TV. A television will provide a very acceptable level of display for graphics and limited text applications and will display the color graphics generated by the PC*jr* in vivid colors.

The optional TV connector and interface cable assembly, plugs into a special connector on the back of the system's unit, and then, through a switching box, directly into the VHF antenna input of the television, as shown in Fig. 4-2. The system is set up for 300-ohm twin lead and may require the addition of a standard 75-to-300-ohm matching transformer. The user then selects the "computer" position on the switch box, sets the TV to either channel 3 or 4 (depending on which channel is not in use in that area and which channel is selected on the TV connector.

Notes of caution. At this point a few notes of caution are in order. Connecting a computer to a home television is not always as easy as the computer vendors would have us believe. First of all, the standard output cable is designed for attachment to standard 300-ohm twin lead. This type of antenna connection is found on most of the TVs presently in use, but "cable ready" sets may have only a coax cable input. In that case the user must provide a 75-to-300-ohm matching transformer (Fig. 4-3). This device

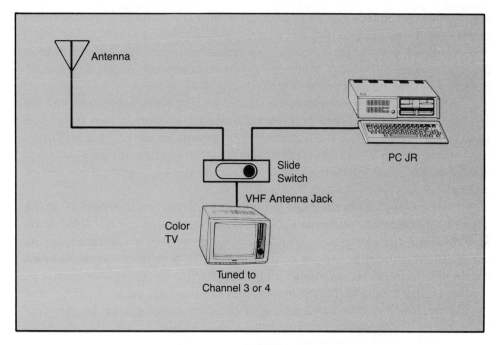

Fig. 4-2. **Installation using a home color TV set
can be very simple and straightforward.**

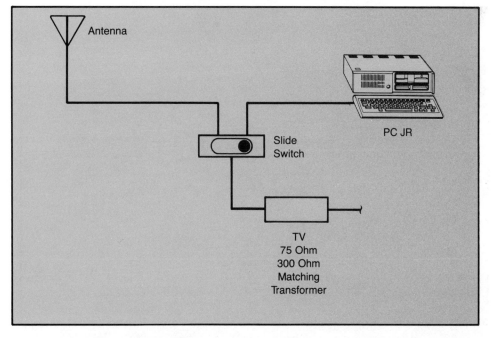

Fig. 4-3. **Connection to home TV with 300-ohm-to-75-ohm adapter.**

screws into the end of the computer cable and then attaches to the screw terminals on the back of the television.

Additionally, if the TV is already connected to one or more outside devices, such as a cable TV system, video disk system, or tape recorder, some additional switching boxes may be required (Fig. 4-4).

Also, note that in connecting the PC*jr*™ (or any other computer) to a TV set that has a master antenna system of any sort, it is important to use the switch box supplied with the TV connection option for the computer. Direct connection to the TV without disconnecting the cable or master antenna system could cause interference to other TVs on the same system for several blocks!

Older color TV sets may not provide the clarity and resolution of the newer ones. Some of these older sets (especially those that are not solid state) may display a picture from the computer that is smeared or distorted. Sometimes turning the fine tuning control on the TV will help, but it is often impossible to improve the picture being displayed.

The entry model of the PC*jr* will support the IBM color monitor or a composite video monitor. Unless family members are fighting for the only TV in the house, however, it may not be wise to spend the additional money

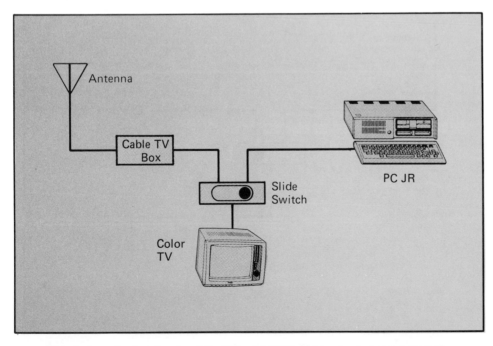

Fig. 4-4.   **A standard cable TV and PC*jr*™ hookup arangement.**

for one of these monitors until you upgrade the PC*jr*™ to the enhanced version.

ENHANCED MODEL DISPLAY

What if you intend to purchase the enchanced PC*jr*™ or want to upgrade your existing entry level unit to the enhanced version? This version of the system will support all the display options discussed in the beginning of this chapter, and a decision must be made as to which monitor is best for your application.

IBM has only one monitor available which will work with the PC*jr*™, the color monitor which permits the full use of color graphics and the display of 80 columns of text. While the quality of the text is not as good as that of a monochrome monitor, it is sufficient for a user whose prime concern is graphics and who also wants the ability to view a full 80 columns of text from time to time.

Another alternative to the dilemma of which monitor to use might be to take advantage of two different options (Fig. 4-5). The design of the system makes it possible to utilize two monitors. For example, if you have a require-

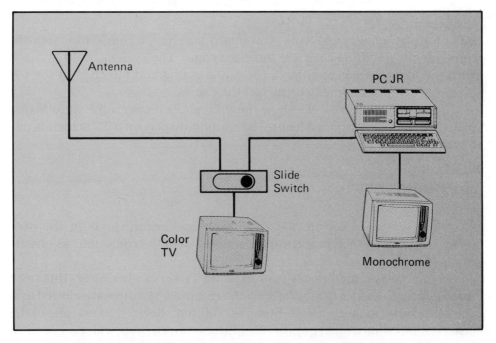

Fig. 4-5. **The PC*jr*™ shown with both a color TV and monitor.**

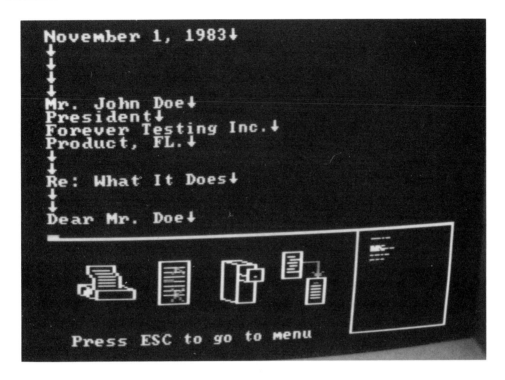

Fig. 4-6.   **Text displayed on the IBM monitor in the 40-column mode.**

ment for high-quality text work, you might purchase a composite monochrome monitor and the color TV interface cable. The system could be used with the monochrome monitor for text processing and attached to the television when it was time to bring out the games.

In figures 4-6 and 4-7 we show the differences between the various displays offered. As mentioned before, 80 column display on a TV screen is not a viable option.

SOUNDING OFF

Since IBM does not provide an internal speaker in the PC*jr*, the user must provide a method of getting the sound out of the computer, as shown in Fig. 4-8.

If you have decided to use your existing TV set as a monitor, this need not concern you, since the audio from the computer is automatically fed into the sound system of the TV. If, however, you have decided to use one of the other methods of displaying the computers output, you will also need to choose a sound system.

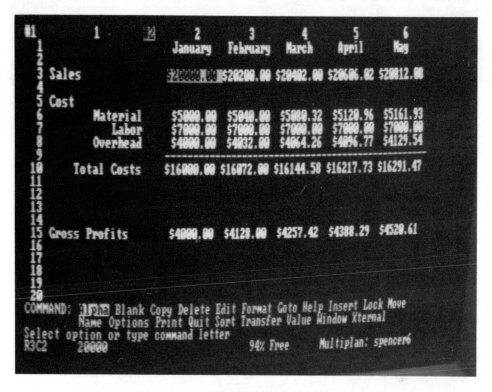

Fig. 4-7. **Text displayed on the IBM monitor in the 80-column mode.**

IBM recommends that, for using the IBM color monitor, you purchase a separate amplifier and speaker to provide sound output. We would like to expand on your options in this regard. It is possible to visit your local Radio Shack store and purchase a small amplifier and speaker. A Radio Shack model #31-1982 amplifier which sells for about $29.95, and a 40-913 speaker selling for about $12.95 will provide more than adequate sound reproduction.

Or, if you want to keep the number of attached accesories to a minimum, you might consider the Radio Shack model 277-1008, self-contained speaker/amplifier combination that sells for about $11.95. There are also several ways to get really big sound from this little machine. The best way is to purchase an adapter that is normally used to take TV sound and feed it directly into your hi-fi system. One of these devices is the teleadapter listing for around $40.00. It is a simple matter to connect the computer output to this device and then to connect it to your stereo. Once this is done, turn on the computer and the stereo and standback. All of the neat sounds that emit from your computer will now be coming at you from your hi-fi speakers.

The final method of providing sound from your PCjr is to purchase a composite monitor that includes a speaker/amplifier circuit. Several man-

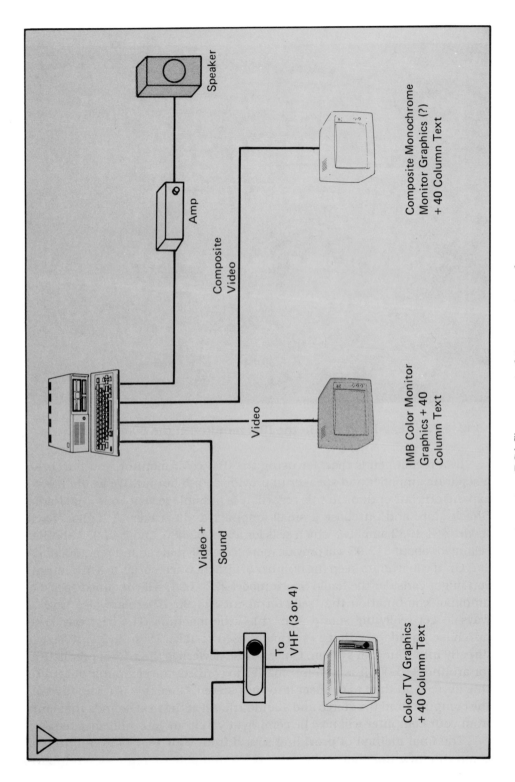

Fig. 4-8. PCjr™ connected to an external amplifier/speaker combination.

Speaker

Amp

Composite Video

Composite Monochrome Monitor Graphics (?) + 40 Column Text

Video

IMB Color Monitor Graphics + 40 Column Text

Video + Sound

To VHF (3 or 4)

Color TV Graphics + 40 Column Text

ufacturers have this type of monitor available including Panasonic, Hitachi, Amdek, and BMC.

I STILL DON'T KNOW WHICH TO USE

Using a color monitor is a double-edged sword. Games, educational software, and text (up to 40 columns) can be displayed more effectively with the enhanced visual capabilities of color monitor. Eighty-column text, on the other hand, is almost unreadable on a color monitor. When viewed on a monochrome monitor, the same 80-column display is sharp and clear. Opting for a color monitor is a valid choice if you intend to use the computer more for its game and educational abilities.

The system supports three types of displays: standard television (black and white or color), a monochrome monitor, or a color monitor.

When used with a television, the computer's output is converted to an RF (radio frequency) signal by the built-in video modulator for presentation to the television receiver. A switch on the converter allows the use of either channel 3 (60–66 MHz) or 4 (66–72 MHz). These are the same TV channels used when connecting a television to most video recorders and cable TV systems. You should use the channel that does not have a TV station on it in your area. There are no areas in the U.S. where *both* channel 3 and 4 are in use except via cable TV systems.

When the PC*jr* is used with a monochrome monitor, which is basically a television set without a tuner, the video signals from the computer are directly coupled to the video portions of the monitor. This results in a higher quality image than possible on a TV. The output from the computer is from a dedicated jack located on the rear panel of the systems housing and is separate from the modulated video output used with a standard TV.

Although connection to a color monitor is the same as for a monochrome display, the actual display is more complex and offers more options than a television or monochrome monitor. The features and complexities of using a color monitor will be discussed along with the applications where they are employed.

The standard display allows for 40 columns by 25 lines of text. A column is the space taken up by a character, such as the letter "a"; in other words, the normal presentation of text will permit 40 characters (including spaces) to be positioned across the screen. This can be expanded to a full 80 columns by 25 lines with an inexpensive add-on module.

FINAL THOUGHTS ON MONITORS

Choosing the monitor that best fits your applications may not be as clear cut as you might like. Because the system has been designed to offer so much to so many (have I heard that phrase before?), the monitor options may lead to confusion. We have talked about many different things in this chapter and so we will spend a few minutes recapping the options here.

If you own or plan to purchase an entry level PCjr™ our recommendation is that you utilize a color TV for the monitor. Even if you need to purchase a 12- or 13-inch portable color TV to use as a dedicated monitor instead of using the one and only family TV, the advantages outweigh the increased cost. First of all, the TV permits the integration of video (picture) display with sound, and secondly, since the entry level system is limited to software provided on cassettes or cartridges, the TV will be more than adequate. Should you upgrade your system as some later time, the TV is still useable for all of the functions with the exception of 80-column text display.

If you start out with, or upgrade to, the enchanced PCjr™ then the type of programs you want to run will dictate the type of monitor you should choose. If your requirments run more to the business side of things than a composite video display capable of displaying 80 columns of text would be the best choice. If you are still primarily interested in programs that utilize color graphics, then a color monitor would be your best bet.

Don't forget that it is an easy matter to use multiple monitors. If you want to have the best of both worlds, a composite monitor capable of high quality 80-column output for word processing and spreadsheet work makes sense. And by purchasing the TV interconnection device, you will still have the ability to use your TV for games and other software requiring color output.

Unless you are sure that using the TV will not satisfy your requirements for a monitor, start with this approach. It is an easy matter to purchase a monitor later and add it to your system. Remember too, that there will be a horde of vendors offering additional add-on products for the PCjr™ within a very short time. It is not possible for us to gaze into our crystal ball and see everything that will be offered, but we can safely predict that the monitor/ sound areas of this system will provide a rich area of endeavor for many of the companies that typically analyze a product, find a need, and then build a new gizmo to meet that need.

You have waited long enough for the arrival of the PCjr™, a few more weeks or months to find the proper monitor to fit your needs will not seriously impair you, and the time spent in front of PCjr™ and the family TV will help solidify your monitor requirements.

CHAPTER 5

IT'S VERY BASIC

BASIC, one of the most popular microcomputer languages available today, is often referred to as an all-purpose computer language. It is flexible enough to be used very efficiently by programmers at all levels and for virtually all applications. As with most spoken languages, BASIC has many dialects. Though a program written in BASIC for one computer may not be directly transportable—that is, it may not run exactly as written on another machine— almost anyone familiar with one variation of BASIC can understand what the program is meant to do. In PC*jr*™'s case, IBM has wisely made the same dialect of BASIC the resident language of the entire PC family, the PC*jr*™, PC, and XT, so that any program written on PC*jr*™ is directly transportable to its big brothers. (Realize, however, that because of memory size limitations, the reverse is not always true.)

The entry of the IBM PC*jr*™ into the world of home computers brings a new dimension to BASIC programming in low cost systems for the home computerist. The PC*jr*™ has a cassette BASIC that is functionally equivalent to that of the IBM PC and XT. This portion of the language (IBM has segmented the language for various purposes) is resident in ROM and provides necessary input/output routines along with high-level support for peripherals, logic, math, and editing functions that make many programs work.

Compared to other BASIC languages available on home computers, IBM's BASIC is extremely powerful. Other home computers have BASIC interpreters on the order of 8K to 12K bytes in length, by contrast, IBM cassette BASIC is 32K bytes in length, and the cartridge BASIC extension is an additional 32K. The amount of memory required for the language itself indicates that, among higher order languages, IBM's version of BASIC has to be considered a strong entry. IBM seems to have thought of everything with this version of BASIC. The language is very "user friendly," and the capabilities are very complete. Most functions are performed directly within the language; in less comprehensive versions, they would require machine language subroutines, direct memory manipulations using peeks and pokes, or not be possible at all.

Cartridge BASIC has features that set the pace for the future home computer market. Several months ago the DISK BASIC on the PC was enhanced with the addition of BASICA or Advanced BASIC. The cartridge BASIC available with PCjr™ adds special macro languages and commands that make programming the graphics and sound functions of the PCjr™ as operator friendly as any to date. Microsoft Inc. was there behind the scenes and deserves credit for much of the developmental work in bringing these new capabilities to the user.

To keep us all speaking the same language, let us clarify the hierarchy of BASIC within the IBM PC family. The PC and XT have a three-level hierarchy: cassette BASIC, resident in ROM; disk BASIC, containing higher level commands and functions used in conjunction with DOS; and advanced BASIC, providing still further extensions to disk BASIC. For the PCjr™, cassette BASIC is functionally the same as its counterpart in the full-sized models. Disk BASIC and advanced BASIC have been enhanced and merged into one segment, cartridge BASIC, which is callable from a ROM cartridge plugged into one of the available cartridge slots.

CASSETTE BASIC

As was mentioned earlier, cassette BASIC is extremely powerful. When you first switch on the computer cassette BASIC is the program in control. You can write your own programs using any of 256 displayable characters, called a character set. Included in this character set are the 128 capital and lowercase letters plus numbers, punctuation marks, and familiar symbols. In addition, international characters and various special symbols used in scientific notations are found in the set.

Joysticks and a light pen can be connected to the system and the inputs from those devices can be interpreted and acted upon by the system. To make these accessories work, cassette BASIC must support certain graphics functions. The graphics support allows you to define points, lines, and even entire pictures if you are willing to stick with it.

One constraint under cassette BASIC is that programs can only be loaded by hand from the keyboard or from a cassette drive since the disk operating system and hence, floppy disk are not recognized by that segment of BASIC. Another constraint is that the PCjr™ will not accept the disk-based extensions of BASIC into memory. Any need for commands or operators from higher levels of BASIC is directed only to the optional cartridge for cartridge BASIC.

CARTRIDGE BASIC

Cartridge BASIC is one of the more exciting features of the PC*jr*™. For anyone familiar with programming under advanced BASIC, the addition of new color graphics options, and the sound macro language will seem like a quantum leap in sophistication. The macro commands available for these new modes will make programming much faster and more effective. This language includes event trapping (interrupts) for activities such as timer, function keys, joystick, etc. Cartridge BASIC is compatible with DOS 2.1 so that programs and files can reside on disk.

The new functions available under cartridge BASIC are:

NOISE: generates noise through the external speaker
PALETTE: allows programmer control of the hardware palette
PALETTE USING: a quick way to set all palette entries
PCOPY: allows coping one screen page to another
TERM: enter terminal emulation mode

This language has innovative commands not implemented in other BASIC languages. Operations can often be performed with a single statement, whereas other BASIC languages require a number of lines of code or even a laborious sequence of "peeks" and "pokes" to perform direct memory manipulations. Cartridge BASIC is another step toward giving complete control of the system to programmers without causing them to labor over assembly language charts and memory maps. It appears that at last a programmer who knows only one language can communicate with the computer. Functions that previously required modification of the operating system or the use of machine language subroutines are now available to the programmer who knows only one language.

Cartridge BASIC can be used without DOS and most commands will still be functional. Disk commands, structured directories, date and time are supported only when DOS is present. Cartridge BASIC requires 6K of RAM for overhead, disk operations with cartridge BASIC require DOS 2.1, earlier versions are not compatible.

DIRECT AND INDIRECT STATEMENTS

When in BASIC the prompt character is "Ok." This prompt means the system is ready to accept commands or statements. A direct command will be performed immediately upon hitting the return key (or ENTER). An indirect command or statement, identifiable by the number at the beginning of the statement, is executed by invoking the RUN command. The list of BASIC statements in memory is executed in sequence starting with the lowest line number. There is a very loose distinction between commands and statements. Generally, "command" refers to operations that are performed in the direct mode and "statement" refers to operations performed in the indirect mode, though most BASIC operators will operate in either mode.

LINE FORMAT

A line in a BASIC program begins with a line number and ends with a carriage return (RETURN or ENTER key). A single line may not exceed 255 characters, including the RETURN. The format for a line would then be:

nnnnn STATEMENT : STATEMENT. . . 'COMMENT   (RETURN)

nnnnn—The line number can be up to five digits in length. It must be an integer in the range of 0 to 65529. Line numbers are always interpreted as decimal numbers, i.e., hexadecimal or other alphanumeric systems may not be used. The program lines are stored in memory by line number and will be executed in that order unless modified within the program by "branch" or "loop" statements. If a line number is omitted, that line will be executed in the direct mode.

STATEMENT—A line may contain one or more BASIC statements. Statements must be separated by colons.

COMMENT—Comments may be included at the end of a line by entering an ' (apostrophe). The characters following the apostrophe are ignored by the program.

ENTERING BASIC PROGRAMS

When the Ok prompt is displayed BASIC program lines may be entered. Using the AUTO command will cause the program to generate a line number automatically after each carriage return, which simplifies the programmer's task greatly. The AUTO command format is:

AUTO linenum, increment [RETURN]

where "linenum" and "increment" are optional parameters.

The automatic line numbering will start at linenum and each subsequent line number will increase by the increment amount. If both parameters are omitted, the parameters default to 10,10 and the numbering starts at 10 and increments by 10. If linenum is specified and followed by a comma without specifying increment, the last increment specified in an AUTO command will be assumed. Consequently, if increment is specified but linenum is not, then line numbering will start at 0. Auto line numbering may be turned off with CONTROL BREAK: hold the Control key down and press the Break key.

Another feature of IBM BASIC allows entry of entire BASIC keywords with simple keystrokes. For example, a ? (question mark) can mean the same as the command PRINT.

$$100 \quad ? \, X \quad \text{is the same as} \quad 100 \quad \text{PRINT X}$$

Other key words can be created by holding the ALTernate key and hitting a letter. For example ALT A is AUTO. Other keywords, generated by holding the ALT key and respective first letter, are shown in Table 5-1.

While entering lines of BASIC code, the features of the editor may be used at any time to correct mistakes or make changes.

PROGRAM EDITOR

The program editor is a line editor that operates on a single line of the program, may include several physical screen lines. For editing a line, the line is first listed on the screen, and then the changes are made. After the changes are made and before the cursor is moved to another line, the enter key (or carriage return) is hit and the entire line is committed to memory. Unless the line number is changed, the new line will replace the old line. If the line number is changed, the old line will be left in the program and the new line will take its sequential position in the program.

Table 5-1   Keywords generated with ALT Key Sequence

Key Sequence	Keyword	Key Sequence	Keyword
ALT A	AUTO	ALT N	NEXT
ALT B	BSAVE	ALT O	OPEN
ALT C	COLOR	ALT P	PRINT
ALT D	DELETE	ALT Q	(NOT USED)
ALT E	ELSE	ALT R	RUN
ALT F	FOR	ALT S	SCREEN
ALT G	GOTO	ALT T	THEN
ALT H	HEX$	ALT U	USING
ALT I	INPUT	ALT V	VAL
ALT J	(NOT USED)	ALT W	WIDTH
ALT K	KEY	ALT X	XOR
ALT L	LOCATE	ALT Y	(NOT USED)
ALT M	MOTOR	ALT Z	(NOT USED)

When editing lines in a program the AUTO line-numbering feature should not be used, since it could create erroneous lines. Each time the Enter key is hit, the program line where the cursor is located will be stored to memory with whatever changes were made. A line may be deleted by typing the line number and hitting the return (this must be done on an empty screen line). If a line does not have a line number, the line will be executed as if it were a direct command. Since program lines may be only 255 characters in length, the editor will truncate anything longer, and the information will be lost.

A number of keys on the keyboard perform special functions that simplify the editing process. Most of these keys are self-explanatory and serve the same function in BASIC editing as their name suggests: BACKSPACE, CURSOR RIGHT, CURSOR LEFT, CURSOR UP, and CURSOR DOWN.

RESERVED WORDS

BASIC has words reserved for its use only, usually abbreviations or contractions. They include the various commands, statements, function names, and operator names used when writing programs. They cannot be used for variable names, since the computer would think that they are to be operated upon: therefore, they are known as *reserved*, or *keywords*. When these commands are to be acted upon, they must be separated from the data or other parts of a BASIC statement by characters permitted within the syntax. Without this *delimiting*, BASIC will not recognize these words. A full list of the reserved words used in IBM BASIC may be found in the PC*jr*™ BASIC reference manual.

NUMBER FORMAT AND PRECISION

Numeric constants, the actual numeric values used in BASIC, may be represented in several ways: integer, fixed point, floating point, hexadecimal, or octal.

INTEGER. Integers are whole numbers (no decimal point) between -32768 and $+32767$. The advantage to using integers is that they require less memory space than fixed or floating point numbers. An integer is stored in two bytes of memory.

FIXED POINT. A fixed point number may be positive or negative and may contain a decimal point. The fixed point number may be either single-precision (seven or fewer digits) or double-precision (eight to sixteen digits). Single-precision numbers require four bytes of memory for storage, and double-precision require eight bytes.

FLOATING POINT. Floating point numbers may be positive or negative. They consist of an integer or a fixed point number followed by an "E" or "D" and a signed exponent. An "E" declares a single precision number raised to the indicated power of 10, while a "D" declares double precision and the exponential value. For example, 17E3 indicates 17 times ten raised to the third power, or 17,000.

HEXADECIMAL and OCTAL. The diehard true programming techy will be pleased to know that BASIC recognizes HEXADECIMAL and OCTAL values. Hexadecimal numbers are base 16. They are indicated by the characters 0 to 9, A, B, C, D, E, and F. Octal numbers are base eight; therefore, characters within the set are 0 through 7. In order to signify hexadecimal numbers within a program, each hex value is preceded by "&H". The subsequent hex value may be up to four digits in length. For example, &H2A, &H123, &HFF45 are all be acceptable hex values within a program. Octal numbers are preceded by "&" or "&O" and may be up to six digits in length. Examples of acceptable octal values include: &123, &O7, and &123456.

String constants up to 255 characters in length are also supported. As with most versions of BASIC, they are set off by enclosing them in quotation marks and must be manipulated by other string functions and commands.

VARIABLES

BASIC recognizes two types of variables, numeric and string. Numeric variables must be number values; in a format as defined above. String variables may be any sequence of letters, numbers, or symbols up to 255 characters in length. If a variable has not been assigned a value, the program assumes that the numeric value is zero or, in the case of string variables, null, which is a string of zero length.

Variable names in BASIC statements may be any length up to 255 characters; however, only the first 40 characters are significant. When naming variables, certain rules must be followed.

- Variable names may include letters, numbers, and decimal points.
- Names must start with a letter but may not start with the characters FN. (A variable name beginning with FN is a user-defined function.)
- Variable names may not be reserved words or reserved words followed by a $, %, !, or #. These symbols are variable type declarations. Reserved words may, however be embedded in variable names.
- Variable names end with $, %, !, or # to declare the type of variable. When a variable is not declared it is assumed to be a numeric single precision variable.

The type declarations are as follows:

$ string

% integer number

! single precision number

double precision number

The following are some examples of variables and their type declarations:

F256#—declares that the value for this variable will be double precision.
ACCOUNTNUM$—indicates a string variable.
COUNT45%—indicates that integers only will be held in this register.
X5 (or any undeclared name)—indicates a single-precision numeric variable.

FILES AND I/O

Under BASIC, information is read or written to files by opening the file (using the OPEN command) by device name and file number. All files are treated as if they were general I/O devices. In cassette BASIC, a maximum of 4 files can be open at any one time. However, the display, keyboard, and cassette are all considered files and are considered open whenever the program is invoked. When using the more advanced cartridge BASIC the default maximum number of files that can be opened is 3, though this can be changed when entering BASIC with the /F switch. By utilizing this feature, up to 15 files may be opened at any one time.

After opening a file, both the file itself and the information contained in it can be manipulated by I/O statements that address that file by number. Conventions for working within the files are the same under PC*jr*™'s cassette and cartridge BASIC as those of the PC and XT. Finally, as with the other versions, files must be closed to write the last information to that file or device; the commands END, NEW, RESET, SYSTEM, or RUN cause all open files and devices to be automatically closed.

OPERATORS

Arithmetic, relational, logical, and string operators, along with the various special functions are the same under cassette and cartridge BASIC as they are under the PC's three segments of BASIC. Besides being compatible with other IBM products, the commands follow standard mathematical convention for order of execution.

GRAPHICS

Remember our saying at the beginning of this chapter that BASIC is known as an all-purpose language? The graphics and sound reproduction capabilities written into PCjr™'s repertoire make this especially true. In most cases we think of programming in BASIC to accomplish some business or mathematical task. The addition of cartridge BASIC to the PCjr™ enhances the world of graphics programming.

Four different resolutions can be selected. With an entry model PCjr™, the only way to take advantage of the color graphics features is by connecting it to your home color TV. You can select either a low resolution, 16-color, 20-column display, or a medium resolution 4-color, 40-column display. In order to take best advantage of the color graphics commands and visual effects, you want either the enhanced version of PCjr™ or the memory and display expansion option installed in the entry model. If this configuration describes your system, your selections, once you are connected to a color monitor, include a medium-resolution, 16-color, 40-column display and a high-resolution 4-color, 80-column display.

In low resolution there are 160 horizontal and 200 vertical points addressable. Medium resolution will double the number of horizontal points, and high resolution will double the number of points again to 640 addressable locations across and 200 down. Points are always numbered from left to right and top to bottom, starting with the upper left corner (0,0) and proceeding to the lower right corner (639,199).

Of course, there are the primary commands of CIRCLE and LINE allowing you to define circles, ellipses, lines, boxes, and the like. Combine with just these two commands the PAINT command and you can fill in the various images that you create. The COLOR command is used to select screen colors in either the text or graphics mode. You can select a background, foreground, and border color for text display and determine a color palette for graphics.

Following are some other commands that fill out the graphics set:

PALETTE and PALLETTE USING—allows you to control palette and pallette colors in use

PSET and PRESET—used when plotting points

DRAW—draws predefined pictures or a complex series of lines and points specified by a string expression; strings may be linked, and the images may be rotated 90, 180, or 270 degrees

PMAP, WINDOW, and VIEW—allows defining of alternate sets of graphic coordinates, converting coordinates between the alternate coordinate set and physical screen coordinates, changing scales to zoom in and out, and defining viewports and windows

These are only a few of the commands available for programming graphics under IBM's cartridge BASIC. Of the commands listed above, only PSET, PRESET, LINE, and COLOR are available under cassette BASIC.

SOUND

As opposed to its brothers, the PC and XT, that have only a small internal speaker and limited sound reproduction capabilities, PCjr™ has a three-voice sound synthesis chip and generates sounds through a special sound driver, using an external speaker (see Chapter 10 for more detail). Cartridge BASIC supports these functions with the Music Macro Language™. Music or sound effects may be programmed in strings, the strings linked, and long complex pieces developed. Using a combination of the PLAY command and interrupts allows you to produce continuous background music or sound effects while a program is running. Additionally, a new command, NOISE, has been added to allow the generation of background noises on the external speaker. This might be useful for sound effects in games.

COMMUNICATIONS

Communications appears to be an important topic to IBM. Cartridge BASIC has commands that aid in accomplishing communications via telephone or RS232C serial interface. A single command, new to IBM BASIC, TERM allows you to enter a terminal emulation mode on the PCjr™. The power of this command may not be fully realized until it is considered in the realm of realtime interface with other computer systems.

INTERRUPTS

Interrupts from several sources can be simultaneously handled under cartridge BASIC. With this flexibility, external devices such as the modem, keyboard, joysticks, or timer can be ignored by the program until the interrupt occurs, at which time the program can branch to special routines. For example, suppose there are two players in a game program, each allocated one minute for his turn at play. In interrupt timer could be programmed to stop the program after each minute and ask for the next player. This is a very useful technique that simplifies programming immensely.

In some dialects of BASIC, for instance, those available in the Apple II or the Commodore 64, event trapping is not supported. Without this feature, the program must be instructed to interrogate the clock, as in the example above, to find out when the given time period (one minute) has elapsed. This can slow program execution considerably if the timer must be sampled, say, every second in order to get an accurate time period.

CHAPTER 6

VAS IST DOS?

DOS is a series of computer programs designed to interface your computer to a disk drive or series of disk drives. DOS (Disk Operating System) provides a way to organize and use the information on disks.

We could say that DOS is somewhat like a traffic cop: it directs all the input and output functions to and from the PC*jr* disk drive. In addition, it permits you to copy files, change their names, verify the information in them, and display them on the screen. The basic purpose of a computer is to run applications, and the DOS operating system is the common thread that allows one to move from one application to another, getting data from one file, writing to another. DOS also provides all of the many housekeeping functions like copying files to diskettes, retrieving files and programs, cataloging the various files on a disk, and keeping track of the amount of space left on a disk. Without DOS, you would have no way of knowing where a specific file was stored on a disk, and the computer would not be able to find it.

DOS is used not only for an IBM PC*jr*™ or other IBM computers but for every microcomputer that has a disk drive. Radio Shack's version is TRSDOS™, Apple's is Apple DOS™, and IBM's is PC-DOS™. The Disk Operating System for the IBM PC was written by Microsoft Corporation specifically for IBM products. Microsoft also has a second version of this disk operating system that is designed for all of the IBM look-alike computers and is called: MS-DOS™ (Microsoft DOS).

The term DOS, as applied to the PC*jr*™, refers to two different things. The Operating System itself consists of a series of instructions that are copied to a disk and read into the computer each time the system is started. The commands for providing various functions are included within these programs. The second part of the whole picture referred to as DOS is the ancillary programs that perform very specific functions when called on by DOS. These programs include the format program, CHKDSK, which checks a disk to see how much space is left on it, DISKCOPY, COMP, MODE, and others. It is really not important for you to know the differences except that the ancillary functions can only be performed if you are using a disk with these programs on it. For example, if you wanted to format a disk and were using a DOS 2.1 master that did not contain the program FORMAT.COM, the DOS, and therefore the computer, would not know how to do this.

Now that we know what DOS is, what are the numbers following it (DOS 1.1, DOS 2.0, and DOS 2.1)? These numbers indicate the release version of the product. Version 1.1 is the oldest one still in use, 2.0 was released when the IBM-XT was introduced, and 2.1 is the newest version and the *only one that can be used with the PCjr*™*!*

As a rule of thumb, a major change in the DOS is accompanied by a major number revision change (1.1 up to 2.0), while a smaller number change indicates that while it is a new release, it does not incorporate many drastic changes, only minor ones to improve its performance or add a few subtle features.

The differences between DOS 1.1 and DOS 2.0 were substantial. DOS 1.1 supported only floppy disk drives and permitted only 320K of storage per floppy. Version 2.0 added the ability to support hard (Winchester) disk drives and changed the disk format to permit the storage of 360K per disk, among other things. The DOS 1.0, the earliest PC-DOS™, supported only 160K of information per disk.

In Chapter 5 you learned a little about BASIC. Some of the commands that were discussed are only supported under DOS 2.0 or 2.1. If you tried to use them under the older DOS 1.1 they would not work. View and Window are two examples of these statements.

THE NEW DOS

Now you know that DOS 2.1 or PC DOS 2.1, to be more correct, is the latest version of DOS, that it was announced at the same time that the PC*jr*™ was announced, and that it is the *only* DOS that PC*jr*™ will respond to. Why is that? The reasons stated by both IBM and Microsoft have to do with what's called disk head settling time. This is the time it takes a disk read/write head to find the proper spot in a disk. Because the disk drive is different in the PC*jr*™ than in either the PC or the XT, the access time is different also.

In order to compensate for this slightly longer disk head settling cycle, DOS 2.1 has been slowed down just a little to permit it to read disks on all the IBM machines. This "slowing down" of the operating system is hardly noticeable and is not important for most applications.

Much has been written in the press about program compatibility between the PC*jr*™ and the PC and XT. Many of the reports conclude that the problems associated with moving programs from one machine to another are the result of differences in DOS. According to MicroSoft this is not true. The only limitations on program portability result from memory limitations within the PC*jr*™ and not the DOS version used.

The PC*jr*™ is not able to use a DOS 2.0 disk. If, however, you copy the program over to a disk that contains the DOS 2.1 operating system, it will run fine. Again, DOS 2.1 is not the limiting factor, the memory size is. Most programs you purchase will come on a disk that contains no operating system. If you follow the instructions provided by the software manufacturer, all you will need do is to format a disk under DOS 2.1 and move or copy the program to this disk.

All the other changes either correct "bugs" that have been discovered in the 2.0 release of DOS or add features of the DOS that were described in the DOS 2.0 manual but had not been implemented. As a side note of interest, Microsoft has already released MS-DOS™ 2.11 to other OEM vendors for use with their systems. DOS 2.11 and 2.1 vary in only one regard. DOS 2.11 implements several European functions including the ability to handle certain monetary and other symbols that are specific to the European market. IBM decided not to include these options in their version of DOS.

HOW DO I USE DOS?

So I need DOS to be able to use a disk drive, but what does it do and how do I use it? Let's take a look at the role of DOS in the overall operation of the PC*jr*™. If you do not have a disk drive and you turn on your PC*jr*™, you will be greeted with a 16-color display and then BASIC will be loaded into the system. If, however, you have a disk drive and DOS 2.1 the computer will look at the disk, load the DOS from it, and then ask you to enter the current date and time. You can bypass these steps by merely pressing the return (ENTER) key, or you can enter the correct time and date.

Why do you want to enter the time and date? It seems such a nuisance to have to do this every time you turn the computer on. The main reason is so that if you are working with a series of files or programs the PC*jr*™ will "date stamp" the disk directory, allowing you to tell at a glance exactly which file contains the latest information. As you update files, the date and time of the last access is automatically written into the disk directory. The danger is that if you do not enter a new time and date on a consistent basis, the advantage of using this feature will be lost.

After you have entered the date and time, you will be given a prompt (A>) on the screen. This means that the computer is ready to execute whichever of the DOS commands you tell it to. Try entering DIR for directory. A list of programs should appear on the screen. These are the programs that are stored on the floppy disk in the disk drive. Careful examination will reveal that each program has a name of up to eight characters that is sometimes followed by an extension of three characters. Some of the most common extensions are: COM, EXE, and BAS. BAS stands for a BASIC file; after a while you will remember that in order to use a BAS file you must first load BASIC into the computer's memory. COM and EXE are extensions for **COM**mand and **EXE**cutive files. These files contain programs or instructions to execute programs.

The conventions for naming files allow you to devise your own special system. Once you know what the "reserve" extensions are, you are free to use another three letter combination of your own choosing. Some applications programs automatically assign file name extensions. For example, a word processing program might add the extension DOC for document to any file created within. If your programs do not assign an extension, get used to doing it yourself. Pick some that make sense to you. A letter to Mr. Jones might be called "Jones.Let" or you might use the three initials of a customer's name, such as "Letter.IBM". The reason for this is simple: if you want to copy a group of files for backup purposes and they all end with the same extension, it is not necessary to tell DOS to copy each one of them by name. DOS has a way of permitting you to copy selected files by using a wildcard character. For example, suppose you have eight files ending in LET. All you do is to tell the computer (through DOS) to copy *.LET. The * means any file name and the LET means ending in LET. To copy all the files at once you could say Copy *.* and DOS would copy all of the files on a disk, one at a time, until it was done.

The next column of numbers shown in the directory is the number of characters in a specific file. This is followed by the date and then the time. A typical directory listing might look like this:

```
COMMAND    COM     17664     3-08-83        12:00P
FORMAT     COM      1664     3-08-83        12:00P
CHKDSK     COM      6016     4-04-83         4:54P
AUTOEXEC   BAT        76    11-14-83         6:31a
BASIC      COM     16256     3-08-83        12:00P
BASICA     COM     25984     3-08-83        12:00P
EDITOR     EXE     48640     9-07-83         4:58P
PCJR       TXT     23879    11-14-83         2:38a
CHAP1      DOC     34567    11-15-83         3:56a
        9 File(s)       136639    bytes free
```

The above disk contains a combination of files, there are 9 files on the disk; and there is still room for 136639 bytes of data. The COM and EXE files are program files; the TXT and DOC files might be text files created with a word processing program, and the BAT file is a "batch" file used to start up a program automatically.

As you become more familiar with the way in which the computer works and with DOS, you will begin to see the logic of this operating system. For now, let's see exactly what you must do to prepare to use a disk drive and DOS.

FORMATTING A DISK

When you walk though the door at home, carrying all of the PCjr™ boxes, books, and software applications you bought at the store, you should also have a box of blank diskettes. These disks are used to store your own data, make backup copies of your programs, and write your data files out to. Before you can use them they must be properly prepared. As they come from the factory they cannot be read or written to by the PCjr™ because they have not been correctly "formatted", that is, they have not been prepared by the computer to write information to them.

If you refer back to the disk directory, you will note a program called FORMAT.COM. This is the program that you use to prepare your disks for use. The IBM DOS™ 2.1 manual provides very clear and concise directions for this procedure, but it is not complicated or difficult. From the A> you merely type: Format A:/S and hit return. A message will then be displayed on your screen:

> Insert new diskette for drive A
> and strike any key when ready

Carefully remove the DOS 2.1 master disk from your drive and place a new blank disk into the slot. Then hit any key: the disk drive will start to whirr and click. After a few moments the message;

> Formatting....

will appear, and then:

> Formatting...Format complete
> System transferred

xxxxx bytes total disk space
xxxxx bytes used by system
xxxxx bytes available on disk
Format another (Y/N)?

will appear. If you only want to format a single disk answer the question with an N; if you want to continue to format the rest of your disks, answer Y. The computer will then prompt you to insert another disk and hit any key to continue.

Once you have formatted your disks, label them and put them away so that you can store information on them later. Lest this become a "how to do it" section on DOS, we will leave you with formatted disks ready to use at this point and go on to discuss some of the other commands built into DOS.

DOS COMMANDS

The IBM DOS manual includes a complete list of these commands. Let us look new at some of the more useful commands that are used in DOS in version 2.0 and 2.1.

CHDIR	Change the directory. It is possible to have more than one directory on a disk.
CHKDSK	Check disk for space used and space remaining.
CLS	Clear Screen. This command will clear the screen but leave the selected foreground and background color intact.
COMP	Compare Files. A handy command that checks the contents of a file against the contents of another file. This is useful after a file copy to ensure that the file was properly copied.
COPY	Permits you to copy files. You can copy from one disk to another for backup or from one file to another on the same disk by renaming the new file.
DATE	Permits you to enter a new date in the computer.
DIR	Directory. This command will display a directory of a disk. It can also be used with several options, including DIR/P, which will give you the directory one page (screen full) at a time.

DISKCOPY	This feature will permit you to copy an entire disk to another one, and it will format the new disk automatically if necessary.
ERASE	This command will permit you to erase a file from a disk.
FORMAT	This is the command you learned about above, used to format a blank disk.
GRAPHICS	This command will print the contents of a graphics display screen on a graphics printer.
MKDIR	Make Directory. Used to make a new directory on a disk.
MODE	This command lets you set the options for a printer or a display attached to the system.
PRINT	Prints files in the background. It permits the printing of files while you are doing other things with the computer.
RENAME	Used to rename a file.
TIME	Shows the present time if you have set it. Otherwise it shows a "default time.".
TREE	Shows all of the directory paths found on a specified disk.
TYPE	Displays the contents of a file on the screen.

There are many more commands and programs associated with DOS 2.1, but these get you started. The best way to learn about a new language (DOS is like a new language) is to practice using it. One of the most important things to remember about the PCjr™ or any computer is that it is a machine, so once you learn how to communicate with it, it will do what you want it to. You cannot hurt the machine, it has no feelings, and it won't call you dumb or stupid if you do not get a certain instruction right the first time. By the same token, it won't be much help in telling you what you did wrong either. Dive in, format a few disks and then try out the various commands. Soon you will find that you are conversing with PCjr™ very easily and having a lot of fun in the process.

CHAPTER 7

THE PRINTED WORD

Printer, that noisy monster that sits next to the computer and makes replicas of the screen on paper. With all the complexities of the computer itself, it is only half of a truly valuable tool until it is connected to what is, in essence, a mere typewriter. Without a printer, the fruits of your labor can only be shared with others when a computer is present; you can compose all the letters and reports that you wish, but no one can read them until the printer does its thing.

And oh, how printers can frustrate you. They will scrunch up paper, print over the edges, skip too many lines (or not enough), or just refuse to do anything until you press the right button. Worse yet, they will not even give you the courtesy of telling you that they are waiting for the button to be pushed. It's not quite as easy as turn the key and drive off the lot, but with a little background, patience, and some time, your printer can work for, rather than against, you.

Just as the PC*jr*™ can accept data from various devices, it can also output information in several formats and through several different ports. The PC*jr*™ supports several different types of printers. What you intend to do with a printer will determine the type of printer that you need for your system.

Just as the PC*jr*™ will send data to different types of monitors it will send data to different types of printers. The selection of monitors is fairly limited, but there are many different types and styles of printers that can be supported by the PC*jr*™. We can divide them into three basic categories.

TEXT PRINTERS

The first is the *thermal dot matrix printer* provided as an option from IBM. This is a low-speed device of marginal print quality that will allow you to print any of the information that is displayed on the screen. It will print all of the normal characters, numbers, letters, and punctuation, as well as a large number of graphics characters used in the printing of graphs, charts, and even maps.

Next are the *impact dot matrix printers* that utilize standard paper. They are called dot matrix because they print a series of dots that make up each character. These printers usually run at speeds of from 80 to 300 cps (characters per second), or about 960 to 3600 words per minute, and they sell for anywhere from $300 to $1500. Their intended purpose is to provide a rapid transfer of information from the computer to the printed page. Since the characters are made up of dots, it is possible to see the dots that make up each character (Fig. 7-1). It is easy to tell when something has been printed on a dot matrix printer because the characters are not as sharp and clear as those typed on a typewriter.

 Fig. 7-1.   **Magnified dot matrix image.**

The third type of printer is the *letter quality* or *daisy wheel* type. Daisy wheel has come to mean the same thing in the computer industry as Cadillac does in the automotive industry ("I have arrived, I have a daisy wheel printer"). The output from this type of printer looks identical to the output from a standard typewriter. This is not surprising, since the technology is basically the same. Using a typewriter, a typist strikes a key which makes a type character or a ball called an element move forward, striking the paper. There is a ribbon between the metal character and the paper, and the impact of the character hitting the paper transfers ink from the ribbon to the paper.

A daisy wheel printer works in much the same way except that the typist hitting the key is really the PC*jr*™ sending a digital code to the printer telling it which key to hit the ribbon and paper with. Also, instead of separate pieces of metal or a ball, the characters are laid out around a metal or plastic wheel and look almost like daisy petals—hence the name. These printers, until just recently, sold for $2000 to $5000. Now there are some that cost as little as $600, but they are usually slower, and the quality is not quite as good as their big brothers'. The more expensive of these daisy wheel printers can output at up to 60 cps (about 720 words per minute), and the less expensive ones can be as slow as 12 to 13 cps (144 words per minute). Even, so, they are faster than almost any typist. Most of these printers print in a bi-directional mode; that is to say, they print the first line from left to right and the next line from right to left.

GRAPHICS PRINTERS

So far we have limited our discussion to the printing of text characters. What if we want to be able to print graphics characters, charts, or graphs? Well, the printer manufacturers have anticipated our desires. Both the thermal and dot matrix printers can also print extended graphics characters. Not all dot matrix printers have this capability, so if you want to be able to print graphics, make sure the printer you choose says it has graphics capabilities. Most daisy wheel printers *do not* have this capability. Therefore, investigate your needs closely before bringing home a printer.

Some dot matrix printers on the market today offer the user the ability to print many different colors for graphs and charts. There are also several different high-speed dot matrix printers that have a second mode usually called "correspondence quality" mode. This means that these printers will slow down (usually to one-third of their rated high speed) and print characters using a higher dot density so that they look more like typewriter output.

THE PC*jr*™'s THERMAL PRINTER

For most purposes, the thermal dot matrix printer designed as part of the PC*jr*™ family of accessories will be your device of choice (Fig. 7-2). It is, like the PC*jr*™, small (approximately 12 inches wide, 3.5 inches high, and 9 inches deep), lightweight (7 pounds), and inexpensive. It will handle either individual sheets, fan-fold, or roll paper up to 8.5 inches wide in its friction feed bed. Designed for a light duty cycle, it does not work at lightning speed compared to other printers. It is rated at 50 characters per second, although it prints in only one direction (unidirectional from left to right), so the real output is about 25 characters per second. Even at that pace, it is equivalent to a typist working at a breakneck speed of 300 words per minute! Considering the uses PC*jr*™ is designed for, it should more than adequately serve most users.

But what is a thermal dot matrix printer? Thermal printing technology has been around for several years. It is a reliable yet inexpensive print mechanism. Most of us have seen or used a hand calculator that prints on special paper. Usually this paper has either a silver coating or a glossy-white smooth texture. Such thermal sensitive coatings, when struck by a hot stylus, create an image. The nuisance and expense of ribbons are eliminated; on the other

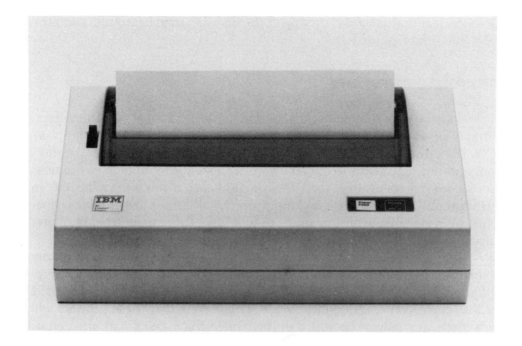

Fig. 7-2.   **PC*jr*™ Compact Printer.**

hand, the specially treated paper is slightly more expensive than paper, and, if you run out, it means a special trip to the computer store where that particular paper is sold.

As for the print mechanism itself, when printing standard text, each character is broken down into a grid, or matrix, 8 dots high and 5 dots wide. The print head is made up of several styli, or hammers, arranged in a column configuration. As the head moves across the paper, appropriate hammers are heated and strike the paper to form letters. An added bonus of this technique is that the hammers can be guided in an almost totally random fashion across the paper (known as all-points-addressable) so that condensed or expanded letters are also part of the printer's repertoire. Another feature of matrix printers is that most, like the PC*jr*™ Compact Printer, are capable of printing graphics, at least within certain limitations.

To get started, you must have both the computer and printer plugged into an AC power source. Only data is sent over the interface cable that connects them, and it is embarrassing to find out that your printer didn't work simply because you forgot to plug it in. Next, connect the interface cable. In the case of the IBM Compact Printer, the cable is permanently attached to the printer, and there is only one slot on the computer that will

Fig. 7-3.   **IBM Graphics Printer.**

accept the cable connector. This is the serial EIA port, which is a modified RS232C connector. This port on PC*jr*™ communicates with the attached device in an industry standard 1200 bits per second (commonly referred to as 1200 baud), 8-bit ASCII format (2 stop bits, no parity). As an option, IBM provides an adapter cable that will permit you to interface other serial printers to the PC*jr*™. Most letter quality (daisy wheel) printers would fall into this category.

Alternatively, a parallel printer adapter option, also available from IBM for the PC*jr*™, will allow you to connect either the IBM Graphics Printer (Fig. 7-3), or a number of other manufacturers' dot matrix units. This optional adapter attaches to the right side of PC*jr*™ and provides a standard parallel output connector.

One special point: unlike the DOS versions 1.1 and 2.0 of the larger PC and XT, DOS 2.1 defaults to the serial printer output rather than the parallel output. You must redirect the output to the parallel printer port if you are using this option. Normally, this means that you must either add a line in the AUTOEXEC.BAT file that reads COM1:=LPT1:, or you will have to enter that command from the keyboard before you begin running a program that you will want to print later.

Are you ready to turn the printer on now? If you are using software other than that known to work in conjunction with your printer, or if your printer is something other than the IBM Compact or IBM Graphics model, do some more reading before you go any further.

In order to perform, the printer has its own memory (ROM), known as a character set. The PC*jr*™'s has the full American 128-character ASCII set plus 63 special characters to permit graphics reproduction. Four text print modes can be selected by commands from the computer:

- Standard—80 characters per line, 10 cpi (characters per inch)
- Double width—40 characters per line, 5 cpi
- Compressed—136 characters per line, 17.5 cpi
- Compressed, double width—68 characters per line, 8.75 cpi

Other commands from the computer select the line spacing that you wish, either 6 or 9 lines per inch.

As you can see, just telling the computer to PRINT is not enough. Most of the commands that go to the printer to control the various modes are almost invisible to you. For example, from a screen menu you may select a compressed print mode in order to get more columns of your spreadsheet on a piece of paper. The computer interprets your request and sends a series of special codes to the printer before sending any of the actual text. In the case of IBM certified programs and IBM printers, these codes should already be part of the program and you should not have to be concerned about them. To get the most out of other programs or to use some other manufacturer's printer, you will have to determine the appropriate codes and insert them in the program yourself.

These command codes may use the ESCape key or the CONTROL key, or they may simply be hexadecimal values. Or if you are programming in BASIC, the printer is controlled in an entirely different way. In any event, the commands are different from standard text information and mean special things to the printer. There are no standardized formats for these codes. It may take an ESCape code to make the IBM printer go into compressed mode, while a printer manufactured by some other company may need a CONTROL code to cause the same effect. To find out just what your printer will do and which codes are required to control the various functions, you will probably have to search through the manual that came with your printer and compare its codes with those identified in your software documentation.

CHAPTER 8

GETTING THINGS STRAIGHT

LOCATING THE SERIAL PORT

Another standard feature of the PC*jr*™, which we have not previously mentioned, is the serial communications port.

The serial port also has another name: *asynchronous communications port.* This means that the serial operation is a series of free running pulses that signal successive instructions. The completion of one set of signals triggers the next, and so on. Since there is no fixed time for each cycle, the actual operation of the port is not related to the operating frequency of the system to which it is connected.

This concept can be difficult to understand, so let's examine it more clearly. The PC*jr*™ is designed to operate at a 4.77MHz clock frequency, over four million clock cycles per second. If you looked at this on an oscilloscope, you would see a steady stream of pulses. Of course we can slow them down to look at each one and analyze it, but it would still be moving just as quickly. This is the frequency for the internal operation of the system, however, and not necessarily for the subcomponents such as the serial port. The serial interface chip, although capable of talking to the rest of the system at the system speed via the bus structure, doesn't talk to the rest of the world that way. Its purpose is to take what's called parallel data and convert it to serial data (Fig. 8-1). This conversion is explained in Appendices B and C.

This conversion naturally takes time. First the data must come in via the system bus, be latched into the appropriate locations, called registers, and be moved out through a different register one bit at a time.

The rate at which the data moves is called the bit rate and the number of signal changes it takes to transmit one bit is called the baud rate. In certain conditions the bit rate and the baud rate can be equal. That means that for every transition, one bit of information is transmitted.

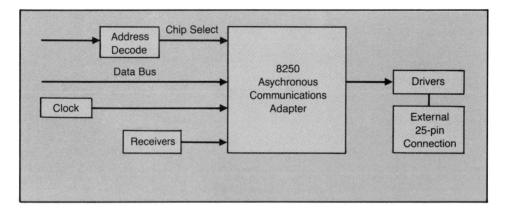

Fig. 8-1. The 8250 asynchronous communication chip
converts parallel bus data to serial data.

Although the two systems that are connected together may be operating
at different internal rates, the serial connection must respond at the same
signaling rate. Therefore, if you decide that you are going to talk to a printer
at 1200 baud for example, you must ensure that both the PC*jr*™ and the
printer serial port are set to the same rate. On the printer, this can usually
be done by flipping some switches or in some cases by sending a special set
of codes.

In asynchronous transmission, each character transmitted is preceded
by a single bit called a start bit. This bit signals the receiving side that a
block of data is coming. The block of data is then made up of seven bits that
define a single character. It is followed optionally by a single bit called the
parity bit. The last bit (or in some cases two bits) called stop bits tell the
receiving side that the block has been sent and instructs it to reset itself to
get ready for more information. When no information is being sent, a high,
or mark, is sent over the data link. The first transition indicates something
is going to happen.

When the receiving side recognizes the start bit or condition, it knows
that it should start counting, looking for a series of bits. When the appropriate length string is received, it knows that a valid character has been
transmitted.

The asynchronous cable adapter is designed to interface the PC*jr*™ to
virtually any RS232C device. IBM provides the following signals: transmit
data, receive data, request to send, clear to send, data set ready, signal
ground, carrier detect, data terminal ready.

HOW THE PORT WORKS

When the 8250 USART device is activated and communications parameters have been established (baud rate, number of start and stop bits, word length and parity), the device is in a *mark* condition.

In relation to actual communications, the mark condition denotes the binary state "1" and the space denotes a "0". As long as the signals are more positive or more negative than $\pm$ 3VDC they are considered valid. Care must therefore be taken not to violate the requirements of the interface by stretching it over too great a distance (50 feet is specified, but RS232C can operate over distances as great as 1200 feet if proper cable is used). The problem is that the signal will be so attenuated (reduced in strength) it may not meet the design requirements for proper operation.

The serial port is designed to operate with the system and BASIC software. The cassette version of BASIC, however, doesn't support communications directly; it requires the use of PEEKs and POKEs to communicate with the port. Cartridge BASIC, which is designed to use some of the functions of the system ROM BASIC and which has hooks to the DISK system, does communicate with either the integrated modem or the serial port.

A new command called TERM has been added to the language that opens up the channel and lets you communicate to the desired port without any special communications packages. Used alone, the TERM command opens a channel to the serial port and sets that port to a minimum operation. This can be changed, however, by redefining the baud rate, parity, duplex mode, filter control characters, whether or not to transmit a carriage return and linefeed, add a linefeed on receiving, and establish the best method of flow control—the ability to stop character flow.

Remember that the commands COM and TERM are only valid with Cartridge BASIC. It is necessary to create a machine language interface in cassette BASIC. Following is a general description of the operation of the serial board with BASIC. See Chapter 5 on BASIC and Chapter 9 on modems for detailed coverage of how to make things work. To use the TERM command, all that is necessary is to type TERM then depress the carriage return. This will cause the PC*jr*™ to default to the serial port.

If you do have the integrated modem in your PC*jr*™, you can establish a double communications link inside the machine. The modem port can be used to communicate to an information source, and the serial port to a serial printer, for example. In that case you must make provisions for buffering incoming data and dumping it to the printer. You can use the Personal Communications Manager software that is set up to handle all of these tasks.

EXTENDING THE PORT

Although PCjr™ has only one serial port, you can extend its capability by adding a switch box (Fig. 8-2). This box, called an RS232C switch, allows you to hook up a number of serial devices and switch between them. Since RS232 switches are asynchronous devices, they are limited to a maximum transfer rate of 19.2K baud.

The switch box is ideal for those applications that require the sharing of very expensive equipment. For example, you might already have a PC or XT and an expensive daisy wheel printer. You can allow the PC and PCjr™ to share the printer by using the RS232C switch box (Fig. 8-3). The switch shown is a manual device capable of handling up to 5 different devices. You could elect to place the PCjr™ as the I/O device and switch it between other units, or you could decide that you want the printer or modem to be available to five other devices and switch the arrangement around.

You can also link more than one switch together to form a matrix that would allow an almost unlimited sharing of peripherals and communication between computers.

One company, Giltronix Inc. of Palo Alto, CA, manufactures a smart switch. Like the internal modem of the PCjr™, it responds to certain pre-

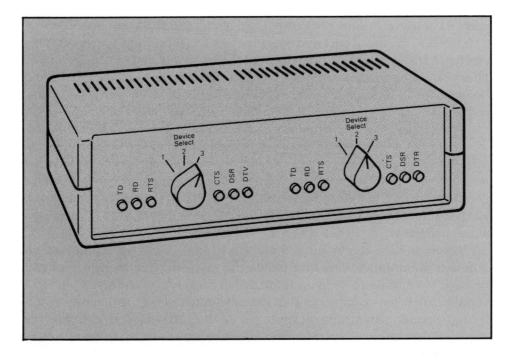

Fig. 8-2.   **Serial switchbox.**

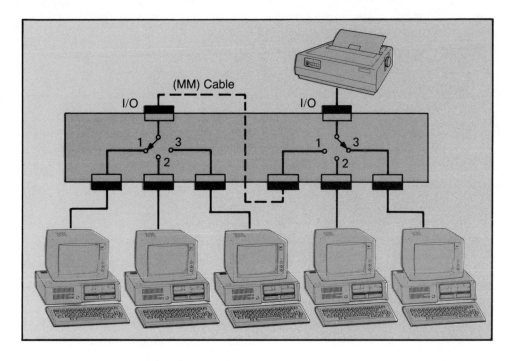

Fig. 8-3.   **Switchbox controls multiple devices, single printer.**

defined codes and is able to store information such as device type. Thus you can establish a setup in which PC*jr*™ can call a specific device simply by using its name.

The serial port is fairly flexible and allows the PC*jr*™ to communicate with other PCs or PC*jr*™s. However, be aware that although the PC*jr*™ and its operation aren't the same as the larger machines, the serial port does provide compatibility of operation and can use most of the existing software. Moreover, the serial communications device on the PC*jr*™ is designed for ease of operation and programming.

CHAPTER 9

TALKING TO OTHER COMPUTERS

The PC*jr*™ is, indeed, a powerful computer, even considered as a stand-alone. But only a telephone call away there are systems that offer hundreds of times its power and storage. When the PC*jr*™ was designed, data communications was planned as an integral part of the system to let two computers "talk" together, just as humans do.

MODEMS

Two computers in the same room can be connected so that data may be transferred from one to the other. If, however, the two systems are located in different locations, thousands of miles apart, how do they communicate with each other? The answer is through the use of modems (**mo**dulator/**dem**odulator). These devices take the computer's output (in the proper format—see Appendix C) and convert it to a series of tones. The modem on the other end receives these tones and converts them back into data bits that can be understood by the computer.

The first modems that became popular in the microcomputer industry were acoustic coupled (Fig. 9-1). The user dialed a number manually using a standard telephone instrument, established a connection, and then inserted the handset into the modem for data transmission. Within the last few years a new modem has emerged called "direct connect," which plugs directly into the telephone line. This direct connection was, until only a few years ago, not permitted by the telephone company. After several long, drawn-out court cases, the Federal Communications Commission decided to permit direct connection of non-telephone company devices to the telephone lines.

It is not necessary for you to become a communications expert in order to allow your PC*jr*™ to communicate with another system. All you need is a

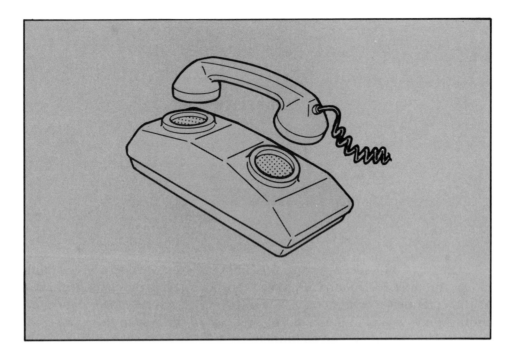

Fig. 9-1. **Acoustic telephone coupler.**

little information about the different formats that can be used when one computer talks to another. You will find a very complete description of these protocols in Appendix C. For now, we will assume that you want to take advantage of your computer's ability to "talk" to another computer. What do you need, and how do you go about setting it up?

The PC*jr*™ has been provided with a special connector on the mother-board to permit the addition of an internal modem for data communications. This modem may be purchased separately and installed simply by plugging it into the proper connector. Next, the user connects the modem to the telephone line with the cable supplied. Most external modems require the use of a serial port. If you use the PC*jr*™'s single serial port to connect a modem, however, you will not be able to connect the IBM Compact printer or any other printer that requires serial connection unless you first discon-nect the modem. The PC*jr*™, since it was designed specifically to support its own internal modem, does not require the use of the serial port when using the IBM modem.

It is not necessary to use the internal modem option (Fig. 9-2) for the PC*jr*™, but it simplifies matters greatly. Installation is very straightforward

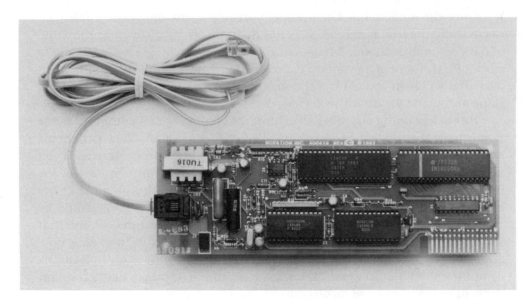

Fig. 9-2. **PC***jr*™ **internal modem.**

and the modem can then be controlled with simple commands. The modem provided by IBM has many features built in that make it an ideal match for the PC*jr*™. Among these features is the ability to dial a number automatically using either DTMF (Dual-Tone, Multi-Frequency: TouchTone™ as it has come to be known), or dial-pulse (rotary dial) dialing. The number to be called is controlled under a software program that will be discussed later. The modem also features an automatic answering mode so that it can answer your telephone when someone else calls in to your computer. It is compatible with Bell 103 type modems (a standard modem first introduced by Bell Telephone) and is approved under Part 68 of the FCC rules and regulations.

Two transmission speeds are supported, 110 baud and 300 baud. (Remember that baud is the speed of the data being transmitted, the number of times per second that the carrier signal is modulated.) At both 110 and 300 baud, the baud rate is equal to the number of bits transmitted per second. (Remember also that for purposes of data transmission, each character is made up of 10 bits, so 110 baud translates to 11 characters per second, and 300 baud to 30 characters per second.) To further confuse you, the system supports only asynchronous transmission, in which each character is "wrapped" with start and stop bits to ensure that the two computers understand each other properly. For a description of sychronous communications, see appendix C.

Once the modem has been properly installed, the telephone cable connected, and the telephone company notified, you are ready to enter the world of data communications. What's out there? How do you get your modem to work? First, there is a program called the Personal Communications Manager that will help you control the modem and data communications functions automatically from the keyboard.

But before doing anything else, have the computer dial a number to see if you have the modem properly installed and connected. This is done by accessing the modem through the communications control software. If you are using The Personal Communications Manager software, first select the interactive mode from the menu and then, using the Alternate (ALT) key along with the "D", instruct the modem to dial a number (this would be represented as ("ALT D"). Choose a number such as the time, or one that you know will not be answered. Let it ring a few times and then pick up a standard telephone receiver. If you whistle a little into the mouthpiece, the computer should start sending back a high-pitched tone. This is the first indication that you have made connection. The tone is very loud and piercing, but that is how computers talk to each other. If you can whistle in ASCII, you can hold a complete conversation with your computer, but since you can't, we suggest that you hang up the phone and type an alternate H (ALT H) to tell the computer to hang up also.

INTELLIGENT TERMINAL

If you and a neighbor both have PC*jr*™'s with the modem option you can dial the neighbor's computer and the two of you can then "talk" to each other by typing information on the keyboard (Fig. 9-3). Whatever you type on your keyboard will be displayed on both screens. Great! Now you can talk between two computers, but is that all there is to a modem?

Bring up the program and you will see a terminal emulation menu that looks like this:

```
     TERMINAL EMULATION MODE

  1. Enter Interactive Mode
  2. Display/Change Comm. Settings
  3. Create/Edit User Function
  4. Save Terminal Options
  5. Load Terminal Options
  6. Print Terminal Options
  7. Display Directory

  Make selection (1-7): [ ]
  Press Esc to exit
```

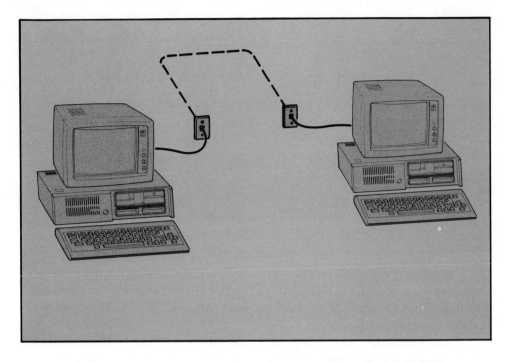

Fig. 9-3.   **PC*jr*™ connected by phone line to another PC*jr*™**

This menu turns your PC*jr*™ into an intelligent terminal. A terminal is the device that is used to talk to computers. Just remember that when computers talk to each other, one will be acting as the computer or host and the other as a terminal. If both computers think that they are hosts, neither will be able to communicate with the other. Conversely, if they both think they are terminals, they won't be able to communicate either. The reason for this is simple. If you dial a host it will answer and send a tone down the line before it hears one. The terminal (your PC*jr*™) will hear that tone and respond with a tone of its own. Once each system has heard the other's tone, you are able to communicate. If you listen to this sequence, you hear the phone being picked up, a tone being sent down the phone line, another tone coming up, and then a sound like the two tones blended into one. At this point you are connected.

Before you do anything else, it is necessary to select option 2 above, Display/Change Comm. Settings. Entering a 2 and hitting the RETURN key brings up the following menu:

```
              Terminal Emulator
         Change Communications Settings

Baud Rate...............................300

Parity.................................Even
Duplex Mode............................Full
Filter control char....................yes
Transmit CR-LF.........................yes
Add LF on receive.......................no
Flow control............................no

Options: (110 300):
```

Since many different formats are used to communicate with a remote computer, this menu will allow you to change the parameters for each call. It is important to match these options with those of the system you intend to communicate with.

In order to help you through this maze, let's start with the number of bits that make up each character. Each character sent and received is made up of 7 or 8 bits, 1 or more stop bits, and parity (see Table 9-1).

As you can see from the table, many different combinations can be used. It is important that you determine the format for each service or computer you wish to communicate with. Fortunately, many of the services use the same setup. If you are not sure which combination is right, try 8, none and 1 (that's 8 data bits, no parity, and 1 stop bit) first. If this does not work, it may be necessary to experiment with the different combinations.

The next parameter that can be changed is the "Duplex Mode" status. Most systems operate in full duplex, but if you start getting double charac-

Table 9-1. Valid combinations for 110- and 300-baud transmissions

DATA BITS	PARITY	STOP BITS
7	MARK	1
7	SPACE	1
7	EVEN	1
7	ODD	1
7	NONE	2
8	NONE	1
8	EVEN	1
8	ODD	1

ters on your *ssccrreenn* when you type, you will need to switch to half duplex (for further information on half and full duplex see Appendix C).

"Filter Control Characters" is a trap that will catch unwanted control characters and discard them. Some host computers may send control characters that are meaningless to the PC*jr*™. If you see extraneous "junk" on your screen, try turning the filter on.

"Add LF (line feed) on Receive" is a setting that will cause the computer to generate a line feed after every carriage return. Typewriters have a return key which generate both a line feed and a carriage return every time it is depressed. Computers permit you to send just a line feed, just a carriage return, or both. Confused? Well, complicated as the description may seem, the solution is really very easy. If, when receiving data from another computer, everything shows up on a single line and writes over itself, you need to turn on the CR-LF. If data is displayed properly, then you don't need to. Conversely, if you get two line spaces between each line of text, turn off the CR-LF. (This would happen if the computer were sending a CR-LF and your computer were also adding a Line Feed after every carriage return.)

In the other direction, the "Transmit CR-LF" command will add an LF each time your computer sends a carriage return. If the person looking at the computer on the other end complains about seeing all your data on the same line, turn this setting on.

Now that the system is all set up for a specific remote computer, let's go back to the terminal emulation menu. From this menu it is possible to save parameters so that you do not have to set them (or even remember what they are) each time you want to call that computer.

You can also setup an automatic log-on system so that your PC*jr*™ can automatically dial a specific service, log on with your sign-on and password codes, get to the specific information you need or want, print it out on the printer or save it to disk, and then sign you off again. Why would you want to do this? You might want to be able to check on the stocks you own each day. By signing up with the Dow Jones service, you can access this system and obtain all the information you want. To manually dial the service, sign on, and then ask for a listing of your stocks each day is a very time-consuming project. If, however, you have set up a series of terminal options to do this automatically, all you need do is load the program and hit a single key! Now, isn't that what a computer is all about?

ELECTRONIC MAIL

Let us look at just one more of the automatic features provided by the modem and software combination. From the main menu, access the "Electonic Mail" menu. You should see something like this on your screen:

```
            Electronic Mail
1. Send/Receive Mail
2. Review/Address Outgoing Mail
3. Review Incoming Mail
4. Address Book Maintenance

Make selection (1-4): []
Press ESC to exit
```

What we have here is your very own post office, complete with incoming and outgoing mail capabilities. This portion of the program will permit you to

- Exchange electronic mail with other computers using the same program
- Distribute (send) mail to more than one mailbox at a time through user-defined mailing lists
- Send or receive mail at any time of the day or night automatically, while in the unattended mode (you don't even have to be there!)
- Send and receive any IBM PC DOS (IBM standard files)

You thought you would need a separate telephone line for your children? Now you can see that you might want to have one for your computer, too. Think of the advantages of having the PC*jr*™ on-line (connected to the telephone line) at all times and being able to receive messages from any other computer. How about setting up a neighborhood system so that your kids can send and receive mail from all of their friends?

Business applications include the ability to access your home PC*jr*™ from your office PC and download a file that you might want to work on at night. Next morning, you could send it back again so it would be there when your secretary gets into work (saves having to cart floppy disks around). What about sending files (messages) from your office while you are at home sick? You can stay in touch and yet be home getting better.

WHAT IS OUT THERE?

There are several nationwide services that provide a user with access to all sorts of things. These systems utilize large mainframe computers and are connected via a series of access lines through a nationwide network of telephone lines. To access one of these systems, you must subscribe to the service. There is normally a startup or initiation fee and then an hourly connect charge. Charges will vary depending on the service and the time of day that you access the system; they can run from a few dollars per hour to $50 or $60 per hour, depending upon the service.

Once you sign up, you are given a local number to call and a sign-on procedure including a password to protect your account from unauthorized access by others. A system such as the Source^{sm} requires that you dial the access number and go through a sign-on procedure before being connected. Once connected, you can access AP and UPI newswires, programs, Dow Jones stock information, shopping by electronic mail, a large data base (much like having your own encyclopedia in the computer), bulletin boards to communicate with others also on the system, and electronic mail that allows you to write and receive letters from other users.

Listed below are just a few of these services accessible via special nation-wide access systems and a short description of each. It is only necessary to call a local telephone number to gain access (once you are properly signed up and have received your account code and password). These networks permit you to communicate with a computer located many miles away though a local telephone number.

COMPUSERVE

- News retrieval from newspapers and newswires
- Personal computing services including software exchange, programming, word processing, and business programs
- Current and historical financial information on major corporations
- Corporate profiles
- Electronic banking
- Entertainment, movie and restaurant reviews, books, theater, interactive electronic games, advice columns, and trivia tests
- Electronic mail service for sending messages to other CompuServe users nationwide
- Home information: nutrition, gardening, home decorating, education, and more; complete with an electronic encyclopedia and electronic shopping

To find out more, you may contact CompuServe in Columbus, Ohio.

DOW JONES NEWS/RETRIEVAL SERVICE

- Business and economic news
- Dow Jones quotes

* Financial and investment services
* General news and information

Dow Jones may be contacted at: (800) 257-5114, or in New Jersey, (609) 452-1511

THE SOURCE℠

* UPI news service with search
* Electronic mail, nationwide
* Classified ads, buy and sell
* Stocks, bonds, money market and mutual fund information
* Electronic travel service, including access to the airline guide and an on-line travel agency to handle ticketing and reservations
* Electronic games and puzzles

The Source may be contacted at (800) 336-3366 or, in Virginia, (800) 572-2070.

These are just three of the many nationwide networks available to you and your PC*jr*™. In addition, many local systems are springing up as fast as wild rice. Many of the computer stores have lists of services available in your location.

OTHER USES FOR A MODEM

Another use for a modem is communication between your PC or XT at the office and the PC*jr*™ sitting on your desk at home. If the computer at work is equipped with any of the popular telecommunications packages, it will be possible for you to access it from the PC*jr*™ and transfer files back and forth. This could be a decided advantage if you want to do some work at home and then transfer the files to your office machine so you may continue working on them Monday morning.

If your company has a mainframe computer that is set up to receive calls from a remote terminal, it is easy to make a call and then have the PC*jr*™ emulate a standard terminal. In fact, one of the sub-menus in the communications software package is designed to allow you to do just that. Once you have set up the emulation mode for the particular computer you want to communicate with, you need only dial the number and start working.

In addition to the large, timeshare systems, there are also many other computer systems available. Bulletin Board Systems have become very popular in recent years that allow you to leave mail for other users, browse through available software collections, read messages concerning hardware and software for sale, or even find a date for next week!

Various clubs and user groups also sponsor bulletin board systems, and members can exchange information regarding a specific computer, a program, or even how to correct a bug one member has found in a specific application. A user group, by the way, is one of the best possible sources of additional information regarding your computer and software programs.

Lastly, if your children and their friends are able to connect their computers together via telephone lines, think of all the fun they will have sending information back and forth, playing checkers or chess, or just chatting. If you think your phone is busy now, just wait until everyone discovers the world of data communications.

MODEMS AND THE FCC

The Federal Communications Commission (FCC) limits the use of modems to protect telephone companies and their equipment. Since the telephone system is designed to handle voice conversations, several problems can develop when sending modulated tones (the output from the modem' down the lines. First, if the tones are too loud, they can interfere with other conversations being carried in the same cable or microwave radio system. Second, they can interfere with the computerized switching equipment used by the telephone company at each of the many switching offices throughout the country.

It is, therefore, necessary to understand a little about FCC regulations and the clout they give to telephone companies. With direct connect modems, the following rules must be followed:

- A direct connect modem may not be connected to a party line or pay telephone
- The telephone company must be notified that an FCC-registered device is being installed
- Repairs must be performed by an authorized service shop

When notifying the telephone company of intention to connect, a user must provide the following information:

- The telephone number to which the modem will be connected
- The FCC device registration number (refer to your modem instruction manual for this number)

- The ringer equivalence (this number is also in your manual and should be something like 0.4B)
- The number of the modular jack to which the modem will be connected (this is the little telephone jack normally installed on the wall by the telephone company). All these jacks have a standard **USOC** number assigned to them. As an example, a USOC-RJ11 jack (Fig. 9-4) indicates a single telephone line installation, and a USOC-RJ12 or RJ13 indicates a multiline installation. Each of these jack numbers ends with either a C or W: the C indicates a baseboard-mounted jack, and the W indicates a wall-mounted jack. If you intend to use a multiple-line system and switch the modem between lines, you must indicate all the numbers that could be used.

You can notify the phone company by calling the local customer service office. To protect yourself, however, you should follow up this call with a letter confirming the information. It is not necessary to wait for a reply from the telephone company (usually they won't even acknowledge your letter), but it is important that you notify them in writing rather than just calling them up and telling them you intend to use a modem. Presently, there is no additional charge for the connection of a modem to a home telephone line, although several of the telephone operating companies have asked for a special rate surcharge.

If you do not have one of the jacks specified above, you should contact your local telephone company and have your jacks converted or have one installed. **Do not connect the modem directly to the telephone system without using one of these jacks.** Regulations require that the phone company provide a "demarcation" point to which they are responsible for service.

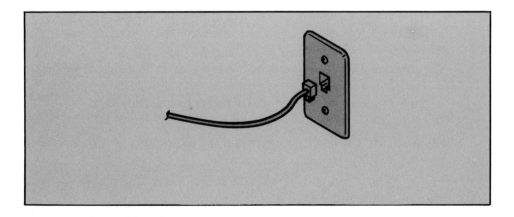

Fig. 9-4. **Wall mounted RJ11 phone jack.**

TALK TO THE WORLD

Now that you understand the power of the PC*jr*™ attached to a modem, you are ready to really enjoy the ability to communicate with the world! IBM has made it very simple for you to experience this world of data communications. But one word of caution: newspapers have been reporting all types of computer abuses with modems and the telephone lines. "Hacking" with systems that you are not permitted to access is a Federal offense and will be punished as such. If you want to try "War Games" in your own living room, be prepared for a knock at the door and a very unpleasant experience. There are enough legitimate uses for a modem without having to find ones that will cause you trouble!

CHAPTER 10

VOICES VOICES VOICES

Among the many capabilities that your PC*jr*™ offers is the generation of tone, sound effects, and music. This chapter tells you about the kinds of sounds you can get from your PC*jr*™ and the additional hardware you may need to use the sound generator.

HOW TO MAKE NOISE

To employ the sound or noise function on your PC*jr*™, you should either connect your system unit to a television set to use its internal speaker or employ an outboard speaker. The external speaker is easily connected to the PC*jr*™ via a jack on the rear panel of the PC*jr*™. If you are using your PC*jr*™ with a monitor rather than the television, you might want to connect this output to your stereo for spectacular results.

Producing sound is a specialized job that requires a dedicated special-purpose sound chip. The chip used in the PC*jr*™ is a Texas Instruments SN76496N complex sound generator.

To produce the sounds, you can use any of the BASICs supplied for the PC*jr*™ or, if you want, 8088 assembly language. BASIC, however, may be the ideal choice, since IBM has gone to the trouble of providing the necessary functions to generate a variety of sounds. They call this the Music Macro Language.™ Included in this unique language are such action BASIC commands as SOUND, PLAY, ON PLAY, and NOISE. The method in which they are combined produces the desired sound effects or music.

In order to understand the process better you might want to explore the sound generator a little more. This device, which is part of the PC*jr*'s™ basic design, is located in the memory map at hexadecimal C0. This is not important if you decide to write everything in BASIC, but for assembly language programmers location is important. Moreover, it gives you an idea of how things are implemented in a sophisticated system like the PC*jr*™.

THE COMPLEX SOUND GENERATOR

The Texas Instruments SN76496N complex sound generator creates sounds in a microcomputer system that are suitable for games, alarms, or just about anything you want sound for. This includes the creation of some fairly sophisticated music programs.

The chip contains three programmable tone generators and a noise generator each with its own attenuator. By using tone generators or combinations of tone generators and noise, an extremely wide variety of sounds can be created. A new BASIC command, "NOISE" has been added to the BASIC language repertoire to take advantage of the noise generation feature of the sound chip.

The chip uses the internal system clock to derive sound frequencies. The PC*jr*™ has a clock that operates at 4.77MHz, for operation of the microprocessor. This clock, however, also provides pulses to the sound generator, but via special timing circuitry so that the sound generator operates in step with the rest of the system. Thus graphics and sound can be coordinated.

In the PC*jr*™ tones are represented by 10-bit binary numbers that determine their frequency and duration. In BASIC this is done by specifying the tone and duration in an English-like statement:

SOUND frequency, duration, tone1, tone2, tone3, volume

Notice that you can mix and combine the tones to make use of all three available tones and the noise. The sound chip has a number of internal memory registers which control the tone frequency, attenuation, and noise type.

The chip input data for the generation of a tone requires two 8-bit bytes. The first byte specifies the tone control register and gives four bits of frequency data. The least significant byte gives the remaining 6 bits of frequency data. The sound registers are cleared by filling them with zeros, otherwise the previous information would be regenerated. This is a plus since for some special purposes you only have to send the information to the chip once and call it many times. Attenuatator control and noise type selection both require one byte of data.

The functions of the sound chip control registers are shown in Table 10-1. The sound chip is also capable of generating either white noise or

Table 10-1. Sound Chip Control Registers

Bit 0	Bit 1	Bit 2	Function
0	0	0	Tone 1 Frequency
0	0	1	Tone 1 Attenuation
0	1	0	Tone 2 Frequency
0	1	1	Tone 2 Attenuation
1	0	0	Tone 3 Frequency
1	0	1	Tone 3 Attenuation
1	1	0	Noise Control
1	1	1	Noise Attenuation

periodic noise that can be varied in length, volume and tone. The BASIC command NOISE is used to create these sounds.

The noise source in the sound chip is a shift register with an EXCLUSIVE OR (XOR) feedback. The rate at which it shifts is dependent on the clock supplied and the noise frequency bits, shown below.

NB0	NB1	
0	0	HIGHER PITCH (LESS COARSE HISS)
0	1	MID RANGE
1	0	LOWER PITCH (MORE COARSE)

A noise control byte controls the noise function and sets the correct internal register.

bit	0	1	2	3	4	5	6	7
	1	R0	R1	R2	X	FB	NF0	NF1

Bits 1, 2, and 3 tell the device that this is a noise byte. Bits 5, 6, and 7 determine the noise type and characteristics. For example a bit setting for a less coarse hissing sound would be:

1 1 1 0 0 1 0 0

In addition to using the noise control byte, the rate at which the noise clock shifts can be controlled by the frequency of tone generator number 3. In this case, the transfer of control is established by setting both noise frequency bits 0 and 1 to a 1. The noise generator can now be varied by changing the frequency of tone generator 3. To perform this in BASIC, key NOISE 1, then SOUND 144,10,T3,V3. This causes the generation of white noise in step with the tone generator.

Not only can you generate varying frequencies for the creation of music but a clock chime can be created as well. The clock chime sound is generated by using two of the tone generators. Tone generator 1 is set to a frequency of 679Hz while tone 2 is set to a frequency of 694Hz, but at a lower amplitude. While tone 2 is held constant and tone 1 is varied in order to create the chime effect. The chime is repeated every time tone 1 is cycled.

You can create sounds ranging from jets taking off to explosions by using a similar technique. For example, the sound of tone generator 3 is run from a low frequency to a high frequency and back again with the time interval between the frequencies increased each time. The result is a sound like a 747 taking off. An explosion is created the same way except the movement of the sound up and back down is varied and clipped at the desired point.

MAKING BEAUTIFUL MUSIC

Tones are sounds of a specific frequency that can be generated at selected volumes (0 to 30) for a specified amount of time (see Table 10-2). The tones are used to make music or sound effects. By using the unique commands in BASIC, SOUND and NOISE, you can create just about any combination you want.

Because the computer executes the BASIC statements as it is making sound, you can create programs that interact with you and the machine at the same time. Further, you can develop special sound effects that add extra excitement to a game. A jet sound, for instance, would make a game with airplanes more realistic.

As explained earlier, you don't have to worry about learning a special language for creating sounds or music. The PC*jr*™'s BASIC language handles it all. Table 10-2 shows you the different frequencies you can use to generate the various notes. By mixing tones, you can create somthing akin to a mini-orchestra.

In Chapter 3, you were shown how to redefine the keys for special purposes. You can, therefore, use a template of a typical music synthesizer to create an overlay for the keyboard, then program the PC*jr*™ to respond as musical tones to each key depressed.

Because the sound generator can handle complex wave forms, thus producing a full range of sound, you can emulate anything from a piano to a flute. Of course this assumes that you have an understanding of music and the combinations of frequencies that distinguish the same note played by different instruments.

Table 10-2. Frequency of Musical Tones

Note	Frequency	Note	Frequency
A	110.00	F	698.46
A flat/B sharp	116.54	F sharp/G flat	739.99
B	123.47	G	783.99
C (low C)	130.81	G sharp/A flat	830.61
C sharp/D flat	138.59	A (above high C)	880.00
D	146.83	A sharp/B flat	923.33
D sharp/E flat	155.56	B	987.77
E	164.81	C	1046.50
F	174.61	C sharp/D flat	1108.73
F sharp/G flat	185.00	D	1174.66
G	196.00	D sharp/E flat	1244.51
G sharp/A flat	207.65	E	1318.51
A (below middle C)	220.00	F	1396.91
A sharp/B flat	233.08	F sharp/G flat	1479.98
B	246.94	G	1567.98
C (middle C)	261.63	G sharp/A flat	1661.22
C sharp/D flat	277.18	A	1760.00
D	293.66	A sharp/B flat	1864.66
D sharp/E flat	311.13	B	1975.53
E	329.63	C	2093.00
F	349.23	C sharp/D flat	2217.46
F sharp/G flat	369.99	D	2349.32
G	392.00	D sharp, E flat	2489.02
G sharp/A flat	415.30	E	2637.02
A (above middle C)	440.00	F	2793.83
A sharp/B flat	466.16	F sharp/G flat	2959.96
B	493.88	G	3135.96
C (high C)	523.25	G sharp/A flat	3322.44
C sharp/D flat	554.37	A	3520.00
D	587.33	A sharp/B flat	3729.31
D sharp/E flat	622.25	B	3491.07
E	659.26	C	4186.01
		C sharp/D flat	4434.92

To organize your PC*jr*™ keyboard, you might consider establishing certain keys to set up note lengths. The top row of function keys may serve well for this purpose. For example F1 might be the length designation ranging from 1 to 9, and F2 could be the octave key.

Next the keys Z, X, C, V, B, N, and M correspond to *do, re, mi, fa, so, la,* and *ti* in the key of C, the white keys on the keyboard. The keys S, D, G, H, and J, on the other hand, correspond to the black keys.

If you set everything up properly, you don't have to enter the length and octave of each note each time it is used, since the keys are set to predefined meanings. You can adjust the tempo and, for the fun of it, display a given note on the screen each time it's depressed.

Although the PC*jr*™ does provide you with a great deal of capability for creating sounds, music, and noise, it's good to have an understanding of how music works. Therefore, you should use a basic music book to learn about music and notes.

CHAPTER 11

SOFTWARE: THE FINAL INGREDIENT

Without software the PC*jr*™ is nothing more than a paperweight. All the fancy hardware in the world won't get you one typed letter or one single hour of fun without the software to handle the word processing or supply the graphics and sound for a game.

IN THE BEGINNING

The first microcomputers to hit the market did not have any software available. If you wanted to turn them into useful systems you sat in front of a series of switches and turned them on and off to program the computer.

The next generation of microcomputers sported a keyboard and a cassette recorder/playback unit. The users could now talk to the computer, write programs, and even save them to a tape; but they still had to write our own programs. If they wanted a game they wrote it; if they wanted a business program they wrote it.

Then came several systems that actually had software programs written for them. These programs were modest at first, but once the industry started to flourish, momentum began to pick up. The first major piece of business software to become available was VisiCalc, an electronic spreadsheet that permitted a user to create "what if" examples using a series of rows and columns. If there is ever a software hall of fame, VisiCalc will be the first member; it sold a lot of microcomputers.

Since all of the microcomputers of the time were based on one of two 8-bit processors (the Z-80 series or the 6502 series), software was written for those two systems and their operating systems. By the time IBM first introduced the PC in July, 1981 there was so much software for the Apple II, Radio Shack TRS-80, and others that you could find virtually any type of program you wanted.

But the IBM PC was a 16-bit system. No software was available for it! People who bought a PC waited for months before they could do anything more with it than show off a few simple games. All the 8-bit software houses meanwhile raced to transport their software to this new world of 16-bit systems. Still, it took over a year for good business and game software to become available.

The next event on the software front was that many of the programmers who were used to writing software for mini computers and mainframes decided that there was gold in the IBM hills! Many powerful software products started to emerge: word processing, data bases, spreadsheets, accounting software, and more. Noticeably lacking from this list were games for the PC. The cost of this machine was high enough that most of the people buying it, at least in the beginning, were not into playing games.

ENTER THE PC*jr*

IBM went about its product introduction of the PC*jr*™ very differently. For months they were working with software vendors and within their own facilities, testing and reworking software so that it would be ready once the PC*jr*™ hit the streets. When the hardware was announced a very complete list of software that runs on the PC*jr*™ was also announced. This may be the first system that had software available before the machine was even available! Scores of programs are already on the street and more are making their way to dealers shelves with every passing day.

One of the advantages enjoyed by this machine is that it has two big brothers in the PC and XT. Much of the software already available for these systems is directly "runable" on the PC*jr*™. Secondly, since many within the industry had been anticipating the arrival of the PC*jr*™ like expectant parents, they were geared up and ready to bring their own products to the market in record time.

FIRST THE BAD NEWS

Before we discuss what programs *will* run on the PC*jr*™, let's get the bad news out of the way. First, the PC*jr*™ will currently support only 128K of RAM (Random Access Memory). The PC and XT, on the other hand, will support 640K to 896K of RAM. Many of the powerful business applications have been written to take advantage of at least 256K of RAM so that they can accomplish their tasks as quickly as possible. Remember that having to access a disk or cassette can really slow down a program.

All of the multi-tasking programs such as Lotus 1-2-3™ and Context MBA™ require more memory than the PCjr™ can muster. Many of the more powerful word processors such as Multi-Mate also require more memory. And the new generation of "wraparound" programs such as DESQ™ and VisiOn™ require at least 256K but run better on systems with 512K of RAM.

Second, the PCjr™ only supports one disk drive. Many of the programs available today require two drives to function properly, especially if the program disk is "protected." Disk protection has gained importance as vendors worry that users will copy their programs and give or sell them to others. To prevent this, they have encrypted the software on the disk to prevent unauthorized copying. Many of these programs require that you place the original program in drive A (the first drive) and the data disk in drive B (the second drive). Since the PCjr™ cannot support a second disk drive there is no way to operate these programs.

Finally, programs written to be supported by other than PC-DOS operating systems will not operate on the PCjr. Both the PC and XT support several operating systems in addition to PC-DOS, but the PCjr™ will not. Therefore, programs written to operate under Pascal™ or CP/M-86™ operating systems will not work.

But, not to worry. Within a very short period of time two things will happen. The software industry will develop software with all the functionality of the "professional software" that will operate within the constraints of the PCjr™. Second, within the hardware industry, IBM and many, many other companies will develop add-on hardware options for the PCjr™ to permit additional disk storage and increased memory usage.

IBM has published a list of software known not to work with the PCjr™, which we reproduce below. Remember that software writers are creative people, so some of these products will be modified to run on the PCjr™. Realize also that the list may not be complete. Too much software is available to come up with a complete list.

SOFTWARE KNOWN NOT TO WORK ON THE PCjr™

DOS 1.1	Fortran Compiler
Basic Primer 1.0	Learning to Program in Basic
Basic Compiler	Peachtree Accounting Software
Fact Track	Monochrome Mazes

Private Tutor	Learning DOS
Typing Tutor	Mailing List Manager
3101 Emulation	Multiplication Tables
Casino Games	Pascal Compiler
Home Budget	3270 Emulation
VisiCalc 1.0 and 1.1	UCSD Pascal
Asynchronous Communications 2.0	APL 1.0
BPI Accounting Software	Cobol Compiler
Decathlon (game)	Time Manager
Fixed disk organizer	

WORDS OF CAUTION

When you walk into a store to purchase software for the PC*jr*™ take the following precautions.

- Do not purchase software because on a salesperson tells you it will work. Check the package or ask for a demonstration on a PC*jr*™! (Software is not returnable in most stores if it has been opened.)
- Make sure that the software package is labeled, "Compatible with DOS 2.1 *and* the PC*jr*™." If it does not say this or something to this effect, do not buy it!
- Make sure that you get software for the specific version of the PC*jr*™ you have. If you have only a cassette recorder and cartridges, do not buy a program that is on a disk. If you have both a cassette recorder and a disk drive, however, it is alright to purchase a program on a cassette, for you can always load it onto a disk.

One last caution: be careful about buying any program that is copy protected. If, for example, you buy a payroll program that is protected so that you cannot make backup copies and if, on payday, the disk develops a problem (and it may), how do you tell your employees that they cannot get paid until you return the bad disk to the software house and get a replacement in a week to ten days? There are other ways to address the problem of software pirating.

WHAT IS AVAILABLE?

Now that we know what software is not available for use on the PC*jr*™, let's take a look at what is. First we will list the software and then we will talk about some of the specific applications.

SOFTWARE KNOWN TO WORK ON THE PC*jr*™

Personal Communications Manager
Juggle's Butterfly
Mouser
Crossfire
Monster Math
Turtle Power
Adventure 1.00
Adventures in Math 1.00
Basic Compiler
Casino Games 1.05
Home Budget, jr.
pfs:Report
Homeward 1.00
Arithmetic Games (set 2.0)
Dow Jones Reporter 1.00
Learning DOS DOS 2.00
LOGO 1.00
Multiplan 1.0 and 1.1
Personal Editor 1.00
Professional Editor 1.00
Word Proof 1.0

Bumble Games
Bumble Plot
Scuba Venture
Mine Shaft
Animation Creation
Adventures in Math
Adventure in Serenia 1.00
Animation Creation 1.00
Basic Program Development
Easywriter 1.15
pfs:FILE
Strategy Games
Arithmetic Games(set 1.0)
Diskette Librarian 1.00
Easywriter 1.10
Learning to Program BASIC
Mailing List Manager 1.0
Peachtext 1.00
Personal Editor 1.00
VisiCalc 1.20

You might notice that some programs appear to be listed both here and under software that won't work. They are, except for the version number following the name. This means that you have to be careful about the version that you purchase.

There are also some programs that will work under DOS 2.1 if the directions provided by either the software vendor or IBM are followed. These directions have to do with properly preparing the disks with the DOS 2.1 operating system on them.

SOME SPECIFIC PROGRAMS

Now that we have developed a list of applications that we know will work on the PC*jr*™, let's take a look at some of them so that we can understand what they are and do. The programs listed below are not being endorsed by us; they are just the ones that we have had time to look at.

HomeWord™ is a word processor program that includes a full screen editor, block copy, and move and delete functions. It also supports Global and selective search and replace commands, partial and full justification (the ability to line up the left margin or both margins), centering, insert, overwrite, and underlining; and the text on the screen is displayed very much as it will look when it is printed out.

Personal Communications Manager™; discussed in detail in Chapter 9, is a program designed to be used with the optional modem. It permits the PC*jr*™ to send or receive any correspondence to or from any compatible computer over standard telephone lines. In addition, it permits you to transmit and receive any DOS-based applications, including spread sheets, charts, graphs, or programs. It also has a mail management system and supports both tone and rotary dialing.

Monster Math™ is an educational game. That teaches addition, subtraction, multipication, and division on six different levels. It features a monster that disappears when the correct answer to a problem is given. The game is done in color with full sound and graphic support.

Next, if you are into designing your own characters to run around on the screen, you might enjoy Animation Creation™, which permits you to create sequences that can be saved on cassette or disk. It features varying speeds, 16 foreground colors, and 8 background colors. There are 254 keyboard characters available and it will work in either 40- or 80-column display mode.

Turtle Power™ is an educational game using a structured programming language that turns the computer into an electronic drawing board complete with sound. You can sketch, change colors, and create tunes. It helps you to learn about computers and includes on-screen help commands.

These are only a few of the programs supported on the PC*jr*™ and we have not even talked about programs on cartridges. Many games that emulate the most popular arcade games complete with sound and dazzling colors are becoming available on cartridge.

WHAT IS AHEAD IN SOFTWARE?

What is in the future for PC*jr*™ software? Despite its memory and disk drive limitations, the PC*jr*™ is one of the most powerful home/small business computers available today. What type of software would you like to see? What game or applications do you need? if you wait a short while someone may develop it. On the other hand, why not write it yourself? Just turn on the system and start:

```
10   REM MY GAME PROGRAM
20   CLS
30   PRINT "WELCOME TO MY GAME PROGRAM"
40   ......
```

The rest is up to you . . .

CHAPTER 12

NOT THE LAST WORD

As you have seen, the PC*jr*™ is a powerful little system. It is the first of a new breed of home/small business computers using a 16-bit microprocessor.

This section is not about the PC*jr*™ as it is today, but rather as we think it will become tomorrow. IBM has long had a history of wading cautiously into new markets and then jumping in with both feet after the water has been tested by others. So it was with this system and the PC before it. When IBM first announced the PC in July, 1981, we believe they were aware that the microcomputer market was growing but unaware of the impact they would have in such a short span of time. They were not used to dealing with consumers or small business operations. They have always operated within the safe environment of the medium to large companies where corporate planning makes actions and reactions more predictable.

The PC met with such resounding success that it caught IBM off guard. We suspect that the PC*jr*™ will meet with this same degree of success, but IBM may be more prepared this time. In fact, we believe that IBM still has some surprises for us in conjunction with the PC*jr*™.

When the PC first was announced the expansion slots were not designated for any specific options beyond the CRT and disk controllers, parallel and serial ports. It was not long, however, before many other companies began to understand that these expansion slots offered many different ways of expanding the PC. As IBM watched, hundreds of cards were developed to fill these slots; even whole expansion chassis were designed with more slots. It shouldn't surprise anyone when IBM announces several new cards of their own to fit into the waiting slots that they so graciously gave to the rest of the industry. But, as with their other products, they will market only those cards and options which have been proven by others to be successful.

With this history in mind, we return to our crystal ball to divine what IBM and others might have have in store for the PC*jr*™.

First, let's look at the rear panel of the PC*jr*™. There is one connector unaccounted for. It is labeled "L" and is labeled "spare." Want to bet? How about L for Local Area Network (LAN), a method by which a number of computers can be connected to and share such devices as hard disk storage, printers, modems, and other expensive options. The present direction in the industry indicates that LANs will be big business for a long time to come, for it makes sense to share both devices and data. You might be working on a project that could use some supporting documentation from the accounting department. Without a LAN system you would have to find the proper file on another compatible computer and then carry a floppy disk back to your own system for use. With a LAN, all you have to do is access the files on the computer used by the accounting department and request the information.

But how would the PC*jr*™ fit into the scheme of things in a LAN? Networking a group of PCs or PCs and XTs together is expensive. Each system costs several thousand dollars, and some of the standard options included with the PC are not really needed in a shared environment. What would you want? A disk drive, some memory, your own low cost printer so that you can see a rough draft before sending a file down the network for printing on the shared printer? It sounds logical. Does it sound like the PC*jr*™? What better way to cut the cost of networking than to furnish work stations at $1200 each instead of $3000 each? Watch for this type of option to spring out of Big Blue before too long.

How about additional memory? The only reason that the PC*jr*™ does not support more memory right now is that it might adversely impact PC sales. Another disk drive could easily be added, but that too would impact sales of the PC.Vendors other than IBM, however, don't care if they lower PC sales or not. Watch for these additions in the very near future: Cartridge-based RAM and a board that replaces the IBM 80-column display and memory expansion board with one offering an additional 256K of RAM, 80 columns, a clock, and perhaps even another serial port.

How about a 300/1200 baud modem to plug into the existing modem slot? It's not hard to do given a little time and a ready market. A hard disk controller? Maybe. How about a videotext setup for the coming boom in videotext transmission on the cable TV systems?

The list goes on and on. We have only thought of the obvious additions to this system. There may not be the expansion slots one finds on the PC and XT, but there are more than enough ways to add devices to this system without them.

Put this book in a safe place, write a note to yourself to open it again in a year, and score our projections. And if you think of something we forgot finish the game program we started for you in chapter 11 and then try your hand at helping the PC*jr*™ grow up!

UNDERSTANDING INFRARED COMMUNICATIONS

This appendix provides a not-too-technical explanation of infrared communications as it relates to the PC*jr*™. An infrared communications link is an invisible, silent, wireless information (or data) transmission. The use of infrared is very common, as you may know, in remote control devices for televisions, video recorders, and other gadgets.

WHAT IS INFRARED?

Infrared is electromagnetic radiation. It is similar to radio waves, another type of electromagnetic radiation used to send information (speech and music) from a transmitting antenna to a radio. The electromagnetic spectrum includes many types of radiation. Others are microwave, x-ray, and gamma ray.

Electromagnetic waves are somewhat like vibrations. In fact, what actually makes one type of electromagnetic radiation different from another is the frequency of its vibration. Infrared is also similar to light, another area of the electromagnetic spectrum. In fact, it is part of what is called the optical spectrum of electromagnetic radiation. The optical spectrum includes infrared, visible light, and ultraviolet. Infrared behaves very much like visible light.

WHY USE INFRARED?

The technology for manufacturing low-cost infrared devices is a fairly recent development. Early remote control devices used ultrasonic (inaudible) sound waves, which are vibrations in air and very different from electromagnetic waves. These devices used special types of reeds activated by a mechanical hammer that caused them to vibrate at specific frequencies. The remote control receiver in the television was tuned to these frequencies and responded by turning on or off or changing channels according to the particular frequency tone that was transmitted. Unfortunately, these devices were so sensitive that jangling of keys often caused the same effect.

As newer devices such as low cost LEDs (Light Emitting Diodes), microprocessors, and detector diodes became available in the electronics industry, ultrasonic remote control devices were replaced by units that operated in the infrared band.

Infrared control units, like those used in the PC*jr*™ keyboard, emit light with a 60° spread. This allows the unit to be used at a range of approximately twenty feet. To avoid conflict with other infrared sources, such as controls for video disk players, stereos, and other televisions, most remote control devices use complex encoding schemes that transmit not only the data, but a device identification code as well. Even still, using a remote control unit for another appliance of the same type in the immediate area will cause interference.

As shown in Table A-1, each type of infrared control device is defined in terms of category and product code. Notice, though, keyboards are as yet undefined. It is believed that the PC*jr*™ keyboard will fall into product group 8, with a new category code of 0111. The code groups, however, will need to be redefined to match the 256 possible keystroke patterns on the keyboard. Thus there is no direct analog on the current product code table.

It is interesting to note that the PC*jr*™ system decoder ROM reportedly uses the available codes 57–64 for special functions. And although there are other unused codes in the existng infrared product code table, the PC*jr*™ will use new device codes for other outboard units.

A SMART OPERATION

Achieving the necessary control with an infrared system requires sophisticated patterns in the emitted light. Therefore, whether it is controlling a television or a computer keyboard, an infrared control unit needs a microprocessor. In the case of the PC*jr*™, the microprocessor is an Intel 80C48. It operates at slightly greater than 2 MHz and has a 128-byte internal memory that is used to store, or buffer, key codes in both the incoming and outgoing data streams.

The Intel 80C48 is an 8-bit device of a class known as CMOS (Complimentary Metal Oxide Semiconductor). CMOS units feature low power requirements and can be operated with batteries. The PC*jr*™ keyboard requires four AA-size batteries when operating in the cordless mode.

In operation, the 62 keys are monitored by the key scanner IC (integrated circuit), Fig. A-1. Each key is matrixed and generates a different bit code, depending on whether or not it is shifted, used in combination with the CONTROL key, or used with a special function key. Five additional bits, called category codes, are added to the key code to define the type of device transmitting the data. See Table A-1.

The cordless keyboard can be thought of as just another serial device. It encodes information in a biphase pulse-modulated stream with each bit-cell a maximum of 440 microseconds in length. The encoded information from the keyboard is sent out serially. The system unit detects the data and sends back a pulse indicating that the bit pattern was received correctly. This process is known as handshaking. At the system unit, the information is stored in a RAM buffer and sent parallel (eight bits at a time) to the address and data bus internal to the machine.

At the keyboard, a code latch is used to hold the key information. An output code switcher turns the infrared LED on and off in the bit sequence that corresponds to the key pressed. For example, keying the capital letter

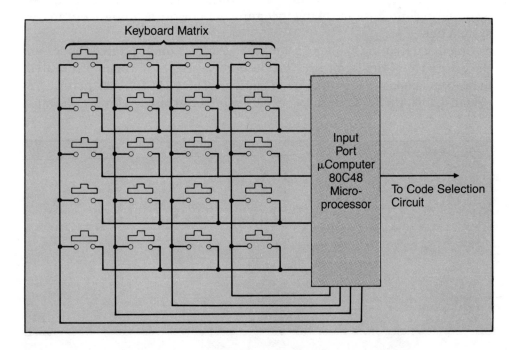

Fig. A-1.   **The 80C48 scans the keyboard matrix.**

"A" (binary 1000001) causes the LED to go from a high to a low with five bit-windows of less than 440 microseconds, and then back to a full-width bit-cell. The 80C48 microprocessor handles all these chores on the keyboard.

The encoding responsibilty is handled by another IC called a character generator. When a key or combination of keys is depressed, the 80C48 looks at the matrix locations and queries the character generator for the proper code sequence, as shown in Fig. A-2. On the receiving side at the system unit, another character generator decodes the pulses. It looks at the first seven pulses for key-code detail, and at the last five for the category code. If everything matches, a character is displayed.

The process can be likened to sending Morse code with a flashlight. Turning the light on and off generates a specific pattern. The same thing happens with the infrared light, except that, rather than actually going off and on, a continuous wave form is sent that changes with respect to time. A pulse with a short duration is considered a binary zero, and a longer pulse (440 microseconds maximum) a binary one. Like any asynchronous data communication, the bit pattern begins with a start bit and ends with a mark or long one. A typical key sequence is transmitted in about 5.28 milliseconds.

In Fig. A-3 you can see how the key matrix works with the microprocessor and the encoding and transmitting circuitry. There are similar circuits on the system unit. However, the system unit is able to operate much faster by buffering and error-checking incoming data before sending it out to the system bus.

As discussed in Chapter 3, the keyboard uses dual infrared diodes on the rear edge of the keyboard that produce overlapping cones of infrared light to encompass the entire line-of-sight view of the PC*jr*™ system unit. To visualize this, the 60° or twenty-foot access area can be thought of as a cone.

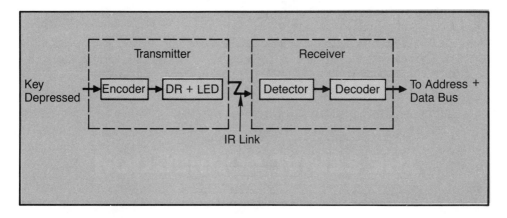

Fig. A-2.   **Transmit/receive sequence.**

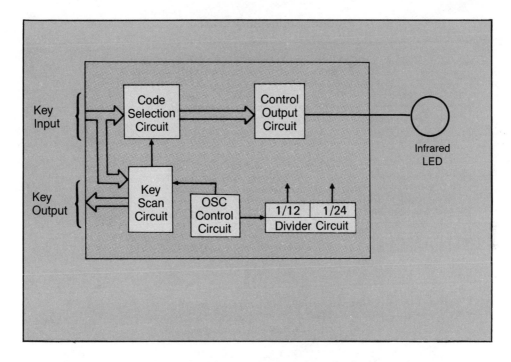

Fig. A-3.   **Multiple circuits work together for keyboard output.**

Table A-1 Product Codes for Infrared Control Devices

GROUP	CODE NO.	CODE	TV 1 0 0 0	CONSUMER VTR 0 1 0 0 0	AUDIO 00001,10001 01001,11001
1	1	0 0 0 0 0 0 0	CH-1/1	CH-1/1	1
	2	1 0 0 0 0 0 0	CH-2/2	CH-2/2	2
	3	0 1 0 0 0 0 0	CH-3/3	CH-3/3	3
	4	1 1 0 0 0 0 0	CH-4/4	CH-4/4	4
	5	0 0 1 0 0 0 0	CH-5/5	CH-5/5	5
	6	1 0 1 0 0 0 0	CH-6/6	CH-6/6	6
	7	0 1 1 0 0 0 0	CH-7/7	CH-7/7	7
	8	0 1 1 0 0 0 0	CH-8/8	CH-8/8	8
2	9	0 0 0 1 0 0 0	CH-9/9	CH-9/9	9
	10	1 0 0 1 0 0 0	CH-10/ (0)	CH-10/ (0)	10
	11	0 1 0 1 0 0 0	CH-11	CH-11	
	12	1 1 0 1 0 0 0	CH-12	CH-12	
	13	0 0 1 1 0 0 0	CH-13	CH-13	
	14	1 0 1 1 0 0 0	CH-14	CH-14	
	15	0 1 1 1 0 0 0	CH-15	CH-15	
	16	1 1 1 1 0 0 0	CH-16 (CLEAR)	CH-16 (CLEAR)	
3	17	0 0 0 0 1 0 0	CH-HIGH (+)	CH-HIGH (+)	CH-HIGH (+)
	18	1 0 0 0 1 0 0	CH-LOW (+)	CH-LOW (+)	CH-LOW (+)
	19	0 1 0 0 1 0 0	VOL-LOUD		VOL-LOUD
	20	1 1 0 0 1 0 0	VOL-WEAK		VOL-WEAK
	21	0 0 1 0 1 0 0	MUTE	X3	MUTE
	22	1 0 1 0 1 0 0	POWER ON/OFF	POWER ON/OFF	POWER ON/OFF
	23	0 1 1 0 1 0 0	NORMAL	EJECT	SCAN SELECT
	24	1 1 1 0 1 0 0	MPX MAIN/SUB	MPX MAIN/SUB	MPX MAIN/SUB
4	25	0 0 0 1 1 0 0	PICTURE-HIGH	STOP	FM
	26	1 0 0 1 1 0 0	PICTURE-LOW	PAUSE	LW
	27	0 1 0 1 1 0 0	COLOR-VIVID	PB	MW (AM)
	28	1 1 0 1 1 0 0	COLOR-PALE	REWIND	SW 1
	29	0 0 1 1 1 0 0	CH-LOCK	FF	SW 2
	30	1 0 1 1 1 0 0		REG	VHF
	31	0 1 1 1 1 0 0	BRT-BRIGHT	REC-STANDBY	UHF
	32	1 1 1 1 1 0 0	BRT-DARK	REC MUTE	REC REVERSE

Table A-1 Product Codes for Infrared Control Devices (continued)

GROUP			TV	CONSUMER VTR	AUDIO
	CODE NO.		1 0 0 0	0 1 0 0 0	00001,10001
		CODE			01001,11001
5	33	0 0 0 0 0 1 0	HUE-PURPLISH	STILL	PHONO
	34	1 0 0 0 0 1 0	HUE-PURPLISH	SLOW-1	TUNER
	35	0 1 0 0 0 1 0	SHARP-UP	SLOW-2 (1/10)	AUX (TV)
	36	1 1 0 0 0 1 0	SHARP-DOWN	SLOW-3 (1/5)	TAPE 1
	37	0 0 1 0 0 1 0			TAPE 2
	38	1 0 1 0 0 1 0			
	39	0 1 1 0 0 1 0	BAL LEFT		BAL LEFT
	40	1 1 1 0 0 1 0	BAL RIGHT		BAL RIGHT
6	41	0 0 0 1 0 1 0	MUSIC VOICE	REVIEW	START
	42	1 0 0 1 0 1 0	SPACE NORMAL	CUE	STOP
	43	0 1 0 1 0 1 0	ANT/NORMAL	ANT-SW	IN
	44	1 1 0 1 0 1 0		FRAME +	OUT
	45	0 0 1 1 0 1 0		FRAME −	CUE
	46	1 0 1 1 0 1 0		ANT-VTR	33/45
	47	0 1 1 1 0 1 0	POWER ON	POWER ON	POWER ON
	48	1 1 1 1 0 1 0	POWER OFF	POWER OFF	POWER OFF
7	49	0 0 0 0 1 1 0		REVERSE	AMS-REW
	50	1 0 0 0 1 1 0		FORWARD	AMS-FF
	51	0 1 0 0 1 1 0		REVERSE x1	PB
	52	1 1 0 0 1 1 0		FORWARD x1	REWIND
	53	0 0 1 0 1 1 0		SWING SEARCH	FF
	54	1 0 1 0 1 1 0			REC-PB
	55	0 1 1 0 1 1 0			REC STANDBY
	56	1 1 1 0 1 1 0			REV
8	57	0 0 0 1 1 1 0			STOP
	58	1 0 0 1 1 1 0			PAUSE
	59	0 1 0 1 1 1 0			
	60	1 1 0 1 1 1 0			
	61	0 0 1 1 1 1 0			
	62	1 0 1 1 1 1 0			
	63	0 1 1 1 1 1 0			
	64	1 1 1 1 1 1 0			

b11 b10 b9 b8 b7	b6 b5 b4 b3	b2 b1 b0
CATEGORY	SET CODE	FUNCTION CODE
STEREO	AMPLIFIER	FUNCTIONS
TV	TUNER	SOUND VOLUME
VIDEO, ETC	ETC	ETC

THE SERIAL CONNECTION

As explained in Chapter 8, a serial interface is another method of adding capability to the PC*jr*™. What we are concerned with in this appendix are the basics of RS232C serial communication.

Serial communication is exactly what you would expect—sending data all in a line. For all practical purposes, the computer sees serial data as a continuous stream regardless of how you set it up for specific communications (see Appendix C).

WHAT IS RS232C?

The term "RS232C" has become a computer buzz word. It is frequently used to mean serial communication in general, but strictly speaking it refers to only one thing: the Electriconic Industries Association (EIA) standard that defines the electrical connection made with a specific connector wired in a certain way, Fig. B-1.

That connector, found on the back panel of the PC*jr*™, is an oblong device designed to connect to a special cable with a plug called a DB-25. This connector is one of the most important on the PC*jr*™; it is the one that matches just about every piece of computer equipment on the market with a serial interface or port.

The particular connector IBM uses is a male DCE (Data Communications Equipment) plug. If you plan to make up your own connecting cable, you will need a female plug, and will need to match the equipment you want to attach to a DCE connection.

Inside the computer, the RS232C connector is wired to a USART (Universal Synchronous/Asynchronous Receiver Transmitter), pronounced *use*

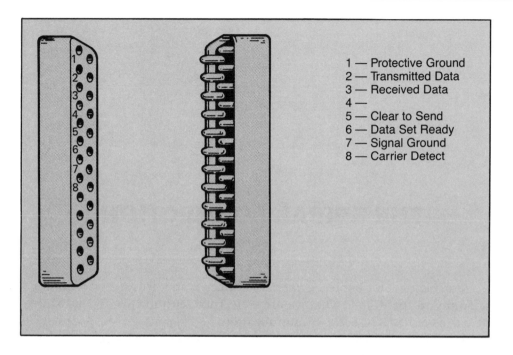

Fig. B-1.   **Standard RS232C (DB-25) connector.**

art. This fancy-sounding device converts eight parallel lines into one, then converts back again, as explained in Appendix C.

A BIT OF HISTORY

Early in the days of data communications, about the time of Wyatt Earp, telegraphs used a much simpler scheme: if a current existed on the line, it caused an electromagnet to bring a metal bar down to produce a click. How the clicks were combined denoted a letter—*Morse* code.

When communications became more sophisticated and greater speeds were required than were possible with a simple telegraph key, the 20-milliamp current loop was born. The current loop, which operated by turning a current on and off in a wire loop, was the method used in Teletype machines.

The advent of computers both created and solved the need for an even more efficient way of transmitting information. As is often the case, computer manufacturers developed a variety of schemes. All the schemes worked, but the problem was that no two pieces of equipment made by different manufacturers would work together. What was needed was a standard method. The EIA, working in concert with the American Telephone and Telegraph

Company and various modem and computer manufacturers, developed a standard for the connection between data communications equipment and data terminal equipment. This standard, called RS232C (the "C" stands for the latest revision), defines the method of interfacing.

Specifically, RS232C covers three areas:

- The electrical signal characteristics
- The functional description of the interchange circuits.
- The subsets of specific interchange circuits.

Each pin on a DB-25 connector serves a specific purpose. In many cases where full capability isn't needed, pins 2, 3, and 7 suffice. They provide a transmit and receive path plus a circuit ground.

Even though RS232C is a standard, it allows a great deal of flexibility. For example, a DB-25 connector is not essential. A smaller or larger connector, or an edge connector on the computer bus structure may be used. IBM has elected to use a special connector on the computer side that is converted with a special adaptor cable to match other devices. The important thing is that the side that plugs into other equipment conforms to the connector type and that the electrical connections match. The important part of the RS232C standard is what each of the functional lines is supposed to do, regardless of the pin assignment or connector type.

These functional lines or interface signals are defined as follows:

Circuit AA—Protective Ground. This line is connected electrically to the frame or chassis of the equipment and provides a path directly to the safety ground of the building that the equipment is in.

Circuit AB—Signal Ground. This is the ground reference used by the interchange circuits. It may or may not be connected. In most equipment such as the PC*jr*™, it is connected in order to match IBM standards.

Circuit BA—Transmit Data. These are the signals generated by the data terminal equipment for the data communications equipment. This circuit is held in a mark (high) condition between characters and when no data is being sent (see Appendix C).

Circuit BB—Receive Data. This is the reverse of Circuit BA above. It is used to send data from the data communications equipment to the data terminal equipment. It operates like circuit BA.

Circuit CA—Request To Send. This signal is used to notify the data communications equipment that information is ready to be transmitted.

Circuit CB—Clear To Send. This is the response to Request to Send. This signal indicates that everything is ready for data to be sent.

Circuit CC—Data Set Ready. This says that the data communications equipment is listening and can handle the data transmission job.

Circuit CD—Data Terminal Ready. This signal lets the rest of the system know the terminal device is ready to handle information. This circuit can be critical for modem operation, since it either puts the equipment on-line or takes it off.

In addition to these circuits, there are twelve more signals defined in the RS232C standard. These special function signals are used when multiple events or special controls are involved, but in typical microcomputer applications they are rarely used.

TIMED BY ITSELF

The method of serial communication used in the PC*jr*™ is called asynchronous. You will learn more about this in Appendix C. It is the least troublesome way to establish communications. In this method, the information is not time dependent; rather, it establishes its own timing by the sequence of information flow. If you looked at this information flow with an oscilloscope, you would see a series of square waves. Each time these waves go from a high—called a mark, to a low—called a space—information is sent. This same sequence occurs regardless of the type of equipment you may be connected to.

In the case of the PC*jr*™ modem, which fits into a slot inside the computer, you don't have to worry about how wires are connected. The only connection that you see is the telephone connector. Internally, however, the signals come from the system bus, an electrical "highway" that lets signals travel to and from different parts of the computer. Control information and information about the address location of the modem and where data should go are all available on the PC*jr*™'s data bus. This internal part of the system is designed to keep track of how the data should be formatted for communication over the data line.

The serial connection itself can be used for communicating with a modem, another computer, or a printer. Care must be taken to connect this cable correctly. For example, if you are communicating with a serial printer, the two most important wires are those on pins 2 and 3. However, to talk to another computer you must reverse the order of these wires.

You now have a pretty good understanding of serial communications, and how to connect different devices. You will find, though, that IBM has taken most of the trouble out of your hands, and all that is necessary is to use the machine.

THE PROTOCOL IS IMPORTANT

COMMUNICATION SENDS THE WORD

There are various ways for computers to communicate with each other or with different devices. Chapters 8 and 9 and Appendix B introduced you to serial and modem communications. On the surface, either form of communication, direct serial or modem, seems simple. And it is simple—if you have everything set up correctly.

Appendix B covered hardware connections for serial communications and explained the standards that define exactly how the physical connections are made. Serial communication also uses specific standards to define the manner in which the information is sent. These standards, called communication protocols, are generally handled in software. They are very much like the rules of order used to run meetings. They establish the order and form in which the information is sent and received.

Even with the most simple communication system, two tin cans and a string, a simple protocol is established. In this example, one speaker decides to speak first while the other listens. Neither tries to talk at the same time as the other, since nothing would then get through due to the simple physics of the transmission.

A similar protocol was established for early radio communications. The speaker would indicate to the receiver that he was finished by saying "over." The receiver would indicate that the information had been received by saying "roger." If a request required an acknowledgment, the receiver would reply "wilco," short for *will comply.* Thus was born the basic protocol known as ACK/NAK (acknowledgment, negative acknowledgment), or handshaking. This protocol is covered in greater detail later.

Of course, the previous examples are simple, but they illustrate the foundations of protocols. When you connect your PC*jr*™ to another microcomputer or call an information service such as The Source^{sm}, some type of protocol must be agreed upon before beginning—who will talk first, who will answer and how, all must be determined.

Other factors in addition to setting up the talker/listener relationship also must be considered.

- How much information will be sent?
- How fast will the information be sent?
- What type of checking will be done?
- Will the discussion be one way or two way?
- Are any special pieces of information required?
- How will the flow be controlled?

The purpose of the communications protocol is to answer all these questions and to ensure the integrity of the connection at the same time. It no longer appears as simple as you might have expected, does it?

Despite all the special requirements, the process by which computers communicate really is simple. In the next several pages, you will learn more about the various protocols and the meanings of terms such as *parity, baud, bit-rate, stop and start bits, message packet,* and *handshaking.*

UNDERSTANDING THE PROCESS

By now you have probably determined that for communication to take place between computers, several elements are required. At the least, these elements include a transmitter, a receiver, and a communications link. As previously explained, the communication link can be a telephone line or simply a physical wire between two computers.

The information that is sent over the communication link is binary in form, which means that only 1s and 0s are sent. You can visualize these 1s and 0s as moving down a pipe, but they are actually electrical transitions that change from low to high and back again, producing a high-pitched warbling sound. The encoding scheme used determines exactly how much information is sent each time the signal changes between high and low. It also defines at what exact point in the signal's transition the information is available. This fact becomes important at the receiving end so that it can be decoded and turned into readable information.

Since data communication uses bits (binary digits) it is logical that groups of these bits would make up specific information. In fact, a single bit can sometimes serve a special purpose in the communication process, but when they are grouped together, they make up transmission codes. The earliest of these codes, used with Teletype machines, is called Baudot; it uses five bits per code. Today, the two most commonly used code sets are ASCII (American Standard Code for Information Interchange), pronounced *as-key*, which was defined by Robert Bemer of Honeywell Corporation in the mid-1960s, and EBCDIC (Extended Binary Coded Decimal Interchange Code), pronounced *ep-se-dick*, developed by IBM for use on their mainframe computers. Both code sets are 8-bit, i.e., they use eight binary digits (1s and 0s) to make up a character or byte.

Although both codes use eight bits, there are not otherwise alike. For example, the letter "A" is represented in ASCII as 01000001. The same letter in EBCDIC takes on a new look, 11000001. Notice that the first bit, known as the most significant or high order bit, is changed from 0 to 1.

Therefore, in order to allow communications between a device that understands ASCII, such as your PC*jr*™, and a mainframe computer that talks EBCDIC, some translation is required. The translation from one code set to another, although not a trivial problem, is easily accomplished inside the computer with the proper software using a technique called a look-up table. Think of a look-up table as very much like the index of this book, but with a sub-index. The computer looks at the incoming bit-stream and determines the bit order. It then compares it to the bit order in the index and makes the proper translation.

MORE ABOUT WHAT HAPPENS

Regardless of how the information is formatted, it must get to the serial line or modem in some way. Inside the computer, there is a device called a USART (Universal Synchronous/Asynchronous Receiver Transmitter). The USART, which looks a great deal like a microprocessor chip, is designed to take information from the system bus inside the machine eight bits at a time, i.e., parallel, and convert it to a serial stream of one bit at a time. Study Fig. C-1. Eight wires come in and one goes out. In computer terms this is called multiplexing.

On the receiving end, the process is reversed. Information comes in serially one bit at a time, and is changed to parallel, eight bits at a time. Of course, the receiving end must also know when to start and stop counting characters (signal transitions). How this is done is discussed later.

The communication channel or data link that connects the devices can be set up to handle data in a variety of ways. One method, called a simplex channel, is used by the familiar newswire or ticker tape. It is designed for

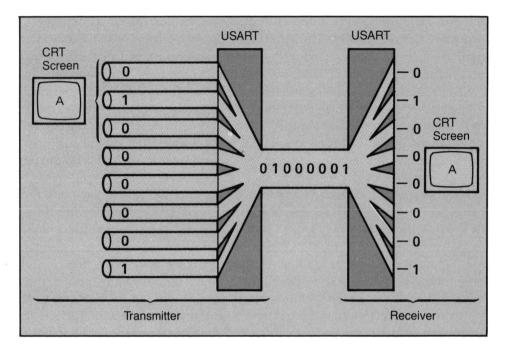

Fig. C-1. **Conversion of parallel to serial data.**

one-way communication only. Another method, called half-duplex, is used in the tin cans and string example. Only one half-duplex transmitter can operate at a time in one direction. The method most often used in communication between computers is full duplex. This method allows both computers to talk and listen at the same time. The ideal way to establish this method of communications is to use four wires. Two wires are used by one device, and the other two by the second device. However, this can be impractical, especially for communications using the telephone network. Therefore, the signals from each machine are usually separated into bands to avoid collisions and still allow full duplex communication.

THE DATA CAN BE GROUPED

As we have seen, information can be sent by grouping it into small clusters or bytes; it can also be grouped into parcels or packets. This is essentially like taking a large document, such as this book, and dividing it up into smaller packages or packets. Data communication packets can be various sizes. Packets of 128, 256, or 512 bytes are typical.

Surrounding each packet is information that tells the communication link the address where it is to go, how long it is, and any special control functions. When communicating with an IBM mainframe, for example, the system may be expecting to communicate with an IBM 3270 terminal. This terminal not only uses EBCDIC to represent data, but has special ways of displaying it on the screen. Thus, the packet information will contain codes that tell the terminal screen to react in a certain manner. The information surrounding the packet also describes exactly how the data is represented and whether any more should be expected. This last element is very important if you're talking to a time-share system with many users.

STAYING IN TUNE AND ON TIME

Communication protocols also determine the manner in which information is sent. There are two main ways to transmit data. They are *asynchronous*, and *synchronous*,. The first method, asynchronous, is used by the PC*jr*™ modem and is typically used with computerized bulletin board systems and most public information networks.

In asynchronous transmission, each character transmitted is preceded by a single bit called a start bit and followed, not surprisingly, by a stop bit. The result is a block of information called a frame. Notice in Fig. C-2 that the rise, or high transition, of the transmitted bit is called a mark. While the level stays high, the transmission is said to be in the idle state. Once a transition to the low state, or space, comes along, it is assumed that a start bit is being sent. Although the length of the idle state, and thus the time between characters, will vary, the receiving computer knows that the start bit signals a flow of eight bits. Most often only a single start bit is used. However, there are times when more than one is used. In those cases, the second start bit allows the system to synchronize with the data flow.

The final bit or bits in the series, called stop bits, signal the end of the character. The purpose of the start/stop bit sequence is to establish the overall timing. Because the transition levels themselves determine the starts and stops, the transmission is not tuned or timed to a specific sequence of events; thus the term *asynchronous.*

Synchronous communications, on the other hand, are time dependent. The information may also be seven or eight bits long, depending on the encoding scheme chosen. Unlike asynchronous communications, there are no start or stop bits. Rather, as shown in Fig. C-2, a special synch character is sent that allows the receiving end to lock on to the data and begin counting each bit until eight are received. Since this form of communication is much

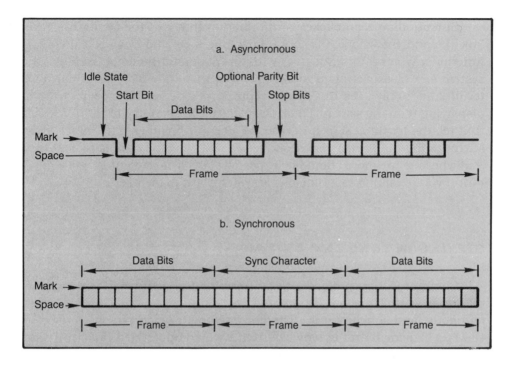

Fig. C-2. **Comparison of asynchronous and synchronous data transmission.**

faster than asynchronous, it is usually used for very high speed transmission between large computers.

Another factor in data communications is parity. Parity is a method of ensuring that data has been transmitted correctly. It is handled by a single bit appended to the end of the data stream. Its predefined condition determines what the computer will interpret as correct. When using parity, the receiving device counts the number of ones in the data stream. If parity is predefined as odd and the number of ones is even, an error is detected. The opposite is true for even parity. Although there are times that no parity is required by either the sending or receiving computer, this condition usually is not satisfactory for communicating over long distances or with a modem.

Even though other methods of error checking exist, such as CRC (Cyclic Redundancy Check), parity is still relied on to determine the nature of the data. Thus when you are connected to another computer, whether directly or by modem, you must ensure that the parity expected by both computers is the same. If it is not, the transmitted information will appear garbled.

GET THE PROTOCOLS RIGHT

One of the reasons protocols were established was to enable two devices to handshake. For computers, handshaking, believe it or not, is very similar to handshaking between people. Both forms show a response to some event. But with computers, it is a little more complex.

Before learning about the handshaking process, you should know that, although data transmission schemes are well defined, the terms explaining them often are not. Such is the case with the word *protocol*. Throughout this appendix, the term *protocol* is used to mean a set of well defined rules that establish the way a data transmission will take place. For the purposes of this text, that definition will stand. However, as we proceed through the next several pages, even that definition will be refined as more information is presented.

The handshaking process is a sequence of acknowledgments that takes place between two pieces of communications equipment. The equipment, as stated earlier, can be two computers, or it can be a computer and a peripheral device such as a printer. In either case, both ends of the communication link have some control of the transmission. This is usually preferred as it allows both the sending device and the receiving device to perform other functions between data transmissions.

Handshaking also allows slower devices to receive data from faster devices. It works something like this

Sending Device: I have data to send to you.

Receiving Device: I'm busy now. Wait.

Receiving Device: (later) I'm ready now. Send the data.

Receiving Device: I'm busy now. Stop sending.

Receiving Device: I'm ready. Continue sending data.

Sending Device: I have completed data transmission.

Without handshaking, the receiving device must be able to accept a transmission at any time, and it must be able to accept and process the data at the speed it is being transmitted.

Part of the handshaking process is the line discipline. The line discipline determines the way data is actually sent and received, how errors are detected and corrected, and in what form the data is grouped. (The term *protocol* is often used to mean the line discipline. In fact, the line discipline is only a part, albeit the most important part, of the total data communication protocol.)

Among the components of the line discipline is what IBM calls SDLC (Synchronous Data Link Control). IBM tells us that SDLC is a bit-oriented, full-duplex (you remember duplex?), serial by bit transmission, centralized control, synchronous, data communications message protocol! That's a lot of words to say that SDLC controls multiple communications and makes sure that they work.

As interesting as all this is, for all practical purposes you don't need to know how protocols work. In most cases, all the communication protocols are taken care of for you by IBM and the other vendors who offer software and modems for IBM equipment. But before we end this appendix, there are a few more minor points you might like to know about.

STOP THAT TRANSMISSION

Most communications protocols provide for stopping and starting a transmission. Generally, the information is captured in an area of memory called a buffer. The receiving device then processes the buffer content and transfers it to a printer or storage device. If the buffer gets full, the receiving device must signal the transmitting device to stop transmitting.

If the receiving device can process the data faster than it is being transmitted, the buffer will never get full. However, when the receiving device is processing data slower than the transmitting device, the size of the buffer determines how often the transmission must stop. For special cases where the processing speed of the receiver and the message size are both known, a system can be devised that requires no handshaking.

Without handshaking, you must make sure that the buffer is big enough to hold the amount of data you will receive. In the PC*jr*™, the buffer size is restricted by a number of factors such as the operating system, BASIC overhead, and any program you may be using.

With handshaking, however, the size of the buffer becomes less important. When the buffer reaches its capacity, a software switch informs the system that it is time to send the data to the desired device. The software also tells the sending device to stop sending data until the receiving computer is ready to receive again. Most printers have this function built in to avoid losing data. You can think of this as a valve on the data pipeline: in order to avoid spilling over, only a certain amount of data is allowed to flow. When the buffer fills up, and a signal is sent to close the valve and stop the flow until the buffer is emptied.

The method of signaling the sending system to turn on and off is also part of the line discipline or protocol. And it is also a part of the handshake process. There are two popular methods: the previously mentioned ACK/ NAK and XON/XOFF. XON/XOFF is the most frequently used, since it is relatively easy to implement. All that is necessary is to send a CONTROL S to stop, and a CONTROL Q to restart. Of course, both sides of the communication setup have to agree which method will be used. In most cases this process is handled automatically by the software; you don't have to worry about it.

As you have seen, although they have many components, communications protocols are fairly simple. And many of the details are taken care of for you by the communication software packages. This appendix is not intended to make you a communications expert, but, together with Chapters 8 and 9 and Appendix B, it should give you a basic understanding of how your PCjr™ communicates with the outside world.

The Motherboard Exposed

This appendix gives you a close-up picture of the PC*jr*'s motherboard on the next two pages. The following list gives a brief explanation of the various components shown in the picture.

Power Supply Board—contains circuitry for converting AC power to proper voltages for internal circuits.

8250 USART—RS232C serial port interface chip.

6845 CRT Controller—converts binary display data to video signals suitable for TV or monitor.

Character Generator ROM—converts binary character codes to display images.

Expansion Slots—internal connectors for accommodating enhancement features; memory and display expansion module, modem, and disk drive adapter.

64K RAM Chips—Random Access Memory chips (8), 64,000 bytes.

ROM—PC*jr*™ resident software; includes disk bootstrap routine, cassette BASIC, diagnostic routines, I/O driver routines, and cassette operating system.

Connector for Parallel Printer Adapter—Connection for externally mounted parallel printer adapter.

8088 Microprocessor—Sixteen-bit microprocessor chip.

8259A Programmable Interrupt Controller—provides interrupt feature (also called event trapping).

8253-5 Programmable Interval Timer—used for timeout functions, time of day, and date.

8255A-5 Peripheral Interface Adapter—programmable input/output device.

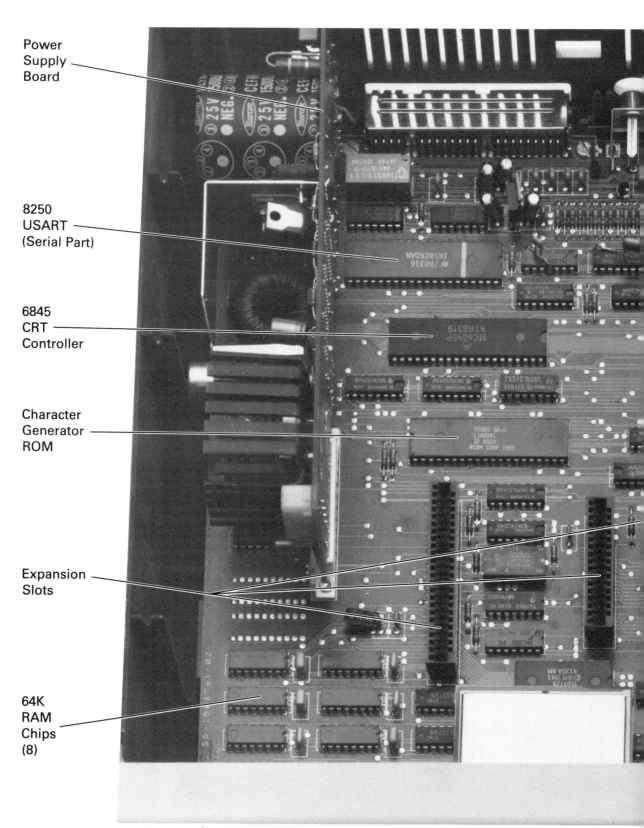

Power
Supply
Board

8250
USART
(Serial Part)

6845
CRT
Controller

Character
Generator
ROM

Expansion
Slots

64K
RAM
Chips
(8)

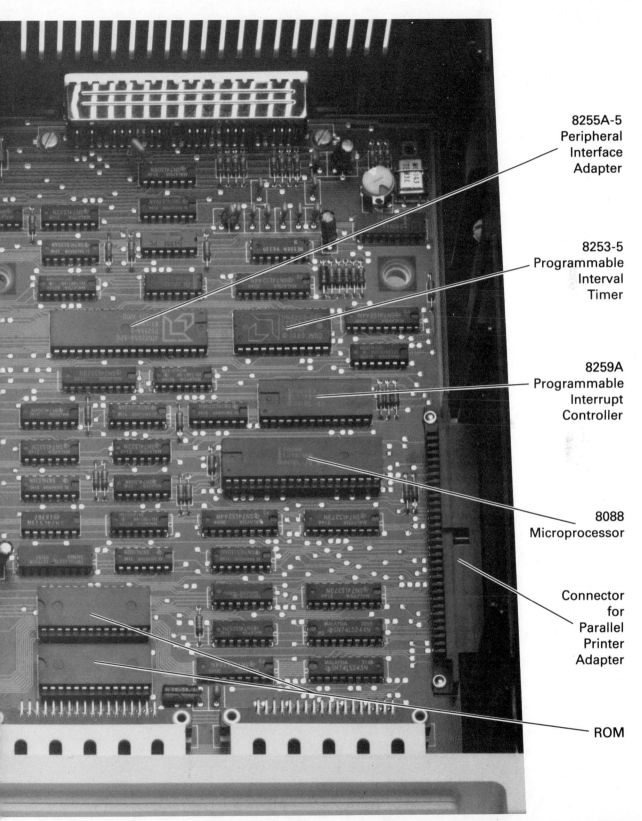

8255A-5
Peripheral
Interface
Adapter

8253-5
Programmable
Interval
Timer

8259A
Programmable
Interrupt
Controller

8088
Microprocessor

Connector
for
Parallel
Printer
Adapter

ROM

GLOSSARY

Getting a book without a glossary is something like going to a ball game and not getting a program. The next several pages will give you definitions of some words that were used in this book and some that are generally useful around computers. The idea is to give you as much information as possible so you can operate and enjoy your PC*jr*™

address A location in the computer's memory that is denoted by a specific bit pattern on the internal system bus. This computer address is like a house address, but it's made up of 20 lines, or bits, which permit the access to one million memory locations.

analog Refers to something with continually variable physical quantities. A good example of an analog device is an ordinary windup watch. As the spring releases its tension, it causes the hands to turn at a specific rate. If you plotted the change of the hands in a 24-hour period you would have a sine wave, a wave that continuously changes from one state to another.

ASCII American Standard Code for Information Interchange (pronounced *as-key*). This standard was developed in the mid-1960s to ensure compatibility between various data devices. It is based on an eight-bit byte of which seven bits are used to define the character. The eighth bit is used for parity, cursor flags, or to define up to 128 additional codes for such things as graphics characters.

BASIC Beginner's All-purpose Symbolic Instruction Code. This is a language that started out simple and grew in complexity and power. The BASIC on the PCjr™, for example, allows graphics and communications and can work with a variety of input/output devices.

baud rate The rate at which information moves between computers. Technically, it is the number of signal transitions per second. But at speeds below 1200 baud, it is essentially the same as bits per second. Since each character takes up 10 bits (8 data and 2 timing bits), 300 baud = 30 characters per second.

binary A system that has only two states, such as on or off, high or low. Thus it has a base of two.

bit The smallest element of information in a computer. The term *bit* stands for binary digit. A byte or character is created by combining eight bits.

buffer A temporary storage area, usually in memory. Normally, a buffer serves an input/output device from a peripheral to the computer and vice-versa.

bus An internal data highway in a computer. The bus is made up of address lines, data lines, and control lines. Options for the computer are normally added by attaching them to the bus, where they pick up signals as well as power.

byte A byte is another way of representing a character. A byte is made up of eight bits. Half a byte, believe it or not, is a nibble.

CMOS Complimentary Metal Oxide Semiconductor. This special type of semiconductor is designed for low-power consumption. For example, the PCjr™ uses an 80C48 microprocessor in the keyboard, thus allowing the keyboard to operate with batteries.

code A set of rules that define how information can be represented in a computer. The code can be machine language or 1s and 0s or English-like statements such as those used in BASIC.

com port Short for communication location. Usually, it is a specific location in memory that the software can locate and send information to and from.

computer Literally, anything that *computes.* Originally, a computer was a person who worked in an accounting house adding numbers. Later, the term was applied to mechanical calculators; today, it is used to mean a stored program device such as the PC*jr*™ that follows a program in its memory to carry out instructions.

CPU Central processing unit, the heart of a computer. For the PC*jr*™, it is a microprocessor—an Intel 8088. Also sometimes referred to as the MPU—microprocessor unit.

CRT Cathode Ray Tube. The terminal screen, or terminal. It simply means the display device, such as a monitor or television.

data The representation of information for use by a program in the computer. It can be a mix of alphanumerics or special graphics codes.

data base manager A special program that puts data in some order and makes it easy to find. There are two types of data base managers: *relational,* in which each part of the data record is related to another part and each record is related to the next, and *hierarchical,* which relies on special lists called indexes and subindexes to locate the data parts and is normally used on large mainframe computers.

data link A technical term for the connection between two devices for the purpose of carrying information.

data processing When computers found their way into modern business in the late 1950s and early 1960s, they were primarily used for taking reams of information (data) and manipulating it to produce reports or bills—hence the term *data processing.* A computer such as the PC*jr*™ performs the same process but in a more efficient and less time-consuming way. Rather than wait days to have the information entered by a keypunch operator, the data is entered directly and the action is usually taken right then.

edge connector An end of a board, such as the disk controller that plugs into the PC*jr*™. This edge has individual gold plated fingers that interconnect the board to the system bus.

graphics   Pictures drawn on the face of the CRT using either special graphics characters that are held in the system ROM, or drawn from point-to-point by addressing the CRT's individual display bits. Graphics can be either high- or low-resolution, depending on the mode of operation and the type of display being used.

handshaking   When computers communicate with one another or with a peripheral device, they like to know that the information got to the other side. The way of doing this is to establish a set of rules where the transmitting end asks if everything got to the other end all right; if it did the receiving side sends back an acknowledgment. This happens every time something is transmitted and thus is called a handshake.

hexadecimal   A numbering system of base 16. It is a convenient way of representing data in a higher form than binary.

interface   a special circuit that allows a device to talk to another device. For example, on the PCjr™ there is a place for a modem interface. This adapts the computer's bus to match the telephone line by adjusting signals and buffering the computer's electrical system from the telephone line.

megabyte   One million bytes or characters.

mode   The method of operation. It can be changed by redirecting operations or changing the characteristics of a specific device.

modem   The word itself stands for MOdulator DEModulator. It takes digital signals from the computer's bus and translates them to analog or constantly changing signals for use on the telephone line, and vice versa.

nibble   Half a byte (no pun intended) or four bits. Used when it is necessary to divide a byte in half to take specific action on the individual bits and then to recombine it into a byte.

parity   A technique that allows information to be checked for accuracy. It may be odd, even, or zero (none).

peripheral   A device such as a modem, printer, or joystick that is attached to the computer and not an integral part of it.

pixel   The smallest addressable item on a CRT. It also has the name *picture element* and is one point or dot on the screen. How many pixels you can get into a cubic centimeter determines the resolution of the display device.

power supply   Whatever supplies the electricity that runs the computer. Most microcomputers require three sets of voltages: $\pm 5V$, $\pm 12V$, and $\pm 25V$. The PC*jr*™ has a unique 60-volt-amp transformer that resides outside the system cabinet. You can think of it as being like the AC adaptor you use with your tape recorder.

RS232C   A standard that defines how a serial communications connector is wired. In addition, it defines specific voltage levels that establish the proper communications.

sector   A division on the track of a disk drive that makes locating the data easier. The PC*jr*™'s disk drive has 40 tracks, each of which is divided into nine 512-byte sectors. The sectors are further divided by sector markers and data headers and end marks.

seek time   The length of time it takes a disk drive to move the read/write head assembly from one track to another. The PC*jr*™ takes 6 milliseconds to perform this task.

INDEX